180 Days of
Spelling & Word Study
for Second Grade

Author
Shireen Pesez Rhoades, M.A.Ed.

Publishing Credits

Corinne Burton, M.A.Ed., *Publisher*
Conni Medina, M.A.Ed., *Editor in Chief*
Emily R. Smith, M.A.Ed., *Content Director*
Véronique Bos, *Creative Director*
Shaun N. Bernadou, *Art Director*
Bianca Marchese, M.S.Ed, *Editor*
Jess Johnson, *Graphic Designer*
Dani Neiley, *Assistant Editor*

Image Credits

All images are from iStock and/or Shutterstock.

Standards

© 2014 Mid-continent Research for Education and Learning
© Copyright 2010. National Governors Association Center for Best Practices and Council of Chief State School Officers.
All rights reserved.
© Copyright 2007–2018 Texas Education Agency (TEA). All rights reserved.
© 2007 Teachers of English to Speakers of Other Languages, Inc. (TESOL)
© 2014 Board of Regents of the University of Wisconsin System, on behalf of WIDA— www.wida.us.

Shell Education

A division of Teacher Created Materials
5301 Oceanus Drive
Huntington Beach, CA 92649-1030
www.tcmpub.com/shell-education

ISBN 978-1-4258-3310-7
©2019 Shell Educational Publishing, Inc.

Table of Contents

Introduction

180 Days of Spelling and Word Study provides the missing piece to today's language arts curriculum. Developed by a reading consultant with more than 20 years of classroom and literacy experience, this research-based program is easy to implement, simple to differentiate, and adaptable to any instructional model. The activities are straightforward and engaging. Most importantly, they address today's college and career readiness standards.

This book boosts students' spelling, vocabulary, and decoding skills by familiarizing them with common patterns in a logical, sequential format. Each five-day unit explores a new concept or letter pattern.

Goals of the Series

The first goal of the series is to build students' familiarity with common spelling patterns and rules. The scope and sequence has been designed using a developmental approach, taking into account students' predictive stages of spelling development. Units progress from basic letter sounds to challenging patterns and spiral from one year to the next.

A second goal is to strengthen decoding skills. When students spend a week or more immersed in a particular phonetic pattern, they start to notice and apply the pattern to their daily reading. This program's emphasis on common spelling patterns strengthens students' word-attack skills and helps them break large words into syllables and meaningful chunks.

Introduction (cont.)

Goals of the Series (cont.)

Vocabulary development is the third, and perhaps most critical, goal of the series. Tasks are meaning-based, so students cannot complete them successfully without some knowledge of the words' definitions or parts of speech. Additionally, activities are designed to deepen students' knowledge of targeted words by requiring them to manipulate synonyms, antonyms, and multiple meanings.

Structured Practice

To be successful in spelling, students must focus on the words, word parts, patterns, and definitions. For that reason, this series uses structured practice. Rather than changing the activities week-to-week, the daily activities are repeated throughout the 36 units. That way, students can focus on the words instead of learning how to complete the activities.

The following activities are used throughout this book:

Title of Activity	Description
Analogies	Students use a word bank to complete analogies.
Homophones	Students choose the correct homophones to complete sentences.
Inflectional Endings	Students add inflectional endings to given words.
Prefixes and Suffixes	Students add a prefix or suffix to given words. Then, they use the new words to complete sentences.
Sentence Completions	Students use a word bank to complete sentences.
Sentence Types	Students use given words to write statements, questions, and exclamations.
Synonyms and Antonyms	Students use a word bank to list synonyms or antonyms of given words.
Turn the Question Around	Students use given words to answer questions in complete sentences. *Turn the Question Around* means restating the question in the answer.
Verb Tenses	Students add endings to given words.
Word Sorts	Students sort words into two categories.

How to Use This Book

180 Days of Spelling and Word Study is comprised of 36 units. Each unit revolves around a particular phonetic pattern and includes five separate activities. They can be assigned as homework or morning work, or they can be used as part of a word work rotation. Activities vary throughout each unit.

In this book, students will explore: long and short vowels, digraphs and blends, silent and soft letters, *r*-controlled vowels, and contractions. Students apply these patterns to one- and two-syllable words and explore vowel teams. Common prefixes, suffixes, and homophones are studied as well.

Unit Assessments

A list of words is provided at the beginning of each unit. The words share a pattern that is reinforced in activities throughout the unit. You may choose to send the words home as part of a traditional study list. Additional spelling activities are provided on page 7. These activities can be specifically assigned, or the whole list can be sent home as a school/home connection.

However, in place of a typical spelling test, you are encouraged to administer the unit quizzes provided on pages 237–238. Each unit quiz contains two words and a dictation sentence. The individual words fit the unit pattern but have not been previously studied. Spelling the words correctly demonstrates that students have mastered the unit's spelling objectives and can apply them to daily work. Further, two to four words in the sentence dictation come from the study list. The rest of the sentence consists of high-frequency or review words. Dictation sentences measure how well students can spell target words in context, while attending to capitalization and punctuation rules.

How to Use This Book (cont.)

Unit Assessments (cont.)

The units are grouped into categories so you can diagnose how well students understand key phonetic patterns. By grouping these units together in this way, you can record the scores for each unit's assessment within a category and better assess student progress. See the Spelling Categories chart on page 239. You may also choose to record unit assessment scores in the Analysis Charts provided in the Digital Resources. See page 240 for more information.

Differentiating Instruction

Once a phonetic category's assessment results are gathered and analyzed, use the results to inform the way you differentiate instruction. The data can help determine which phonetic patterns are the most difficult for students and which students need additional instructional support and continued practice.

Whole-Class Support

The results of the diagnostic analysis may show that the entire class is struggling with certain phonetic patterns. If they have been taught in the past, this indicates that further instruction or reteaching is necessary. If these patterns have not been taught in the past, this data is a great preassessment and may demonstrate that students do not have a working knowledge of the weekly pattern. Thus, careful planning for reintroducing the words or patterns may be required.

Small-Group or Individual Support

The results of the diagnostic analysis may also show that an individual student or a small group of students is struggling with certain spelling patterns. If these patterns have been taught in the past, this indicates that further instruction or reteaching is necessary. Consider pulling these students aside to instruct them further while others are working independently. Students may also benefit from extra practice using spelling games or computer-based resources.

You can also use the results to help identify proficient individual students or groups of students who are ready for enrichment or above-level spelling instruction. These students may benefit from independent learning contracts or more challenging words. The Additional Spelling Activities chart has strong options to further challenge students (page 7 and in the Digital Resources).

Included in the Digital Resources are lists of words used in *180 Days of Spelling and Word Study* for grades 1 and 3. These lists can be used for differentiation. See page 240 for more information.

How to Use This Book (cont.)

Additional Spelling Activities

The activities included here offer additional ways to practice the spelling words in each unit. They also make a great school-home connection!

Activity Name	Description
ABC Order	Write each word on a separate slip of paper. Mix up the slips of paper, and arrange them in ABC order.
Air Spelling	Spell each word in the air using one or two fingers. Have a partner guess which word you spelled.
Best Writing	Write each spelling word two times in your best printing.
Cut Out Words	Cut out letters from newspapers or magazines and use the letters to form the spelling words. Glue the words onto a sheet of paper.
Mnemonic Sentences	Write a mnemonic sentence for each spelling word. For example, a sentence for the word *first* could be: *Fred is racing scooters tomorrow*.
Rainbow Spelling	Write each word with a crayon. Trace around the words in a different color crayon. Trace around both colors in a third color.
Silly Spelling Story	Write a silly story with a beginning, middle, and end that uses as many spelling words as possible.
Spelling Charades	Act out a spelling word. The first person to correctly guess and spell the word gets to act out the next word.
Spelling Hangman	Create a sentence using two or more spelling words. Play hangman until another person solves the puzzle.
Spelling Poem	Write a poem using as many spelling words as possible.
Spelling Scramble	Write each spelling word on a separate index card. Cut apart the letters of each word. Place the letters for each word in a separate zip-top bag. Working with a partner, dump out the letters from one bag at a time and unscramble the words.

How to Use This Book (cont.)

Word Lists

This chart lists the words and phonetic patterns covered in each unit.

Unit	Words	Spelling Pattern
1	ask, blast, cast, clasp, fact, fast, last, mask, past, task	short *a* words
2	bland, damp, hand, lamp, land, pants, plant, slant, stamp, stand	more short *a* words
3	gift, hint, lift, list, milk, mist, quilt, risk, squint, twist	short *i* words
4	best, blend, desk, felt, help, left, next, slept, spend, went	short *e* words
5	blunt, does, dusk, fond, jump, just, must, pond, stomp, stump	short *o* and short *u* words
6	black, click, clock, flock, pluck, smock, snack, speck, stack, stick	–*ck* ending
7	knelt, knit, knob, knock, knot, lamb, numb, wrap, wreck, wrist	silent letters
8	flake, knife, plate, skate, slide, smile, snake, stale, state, write	long *a* and long *i* ending in silent *e*
9	close, flute, globe, plume, slope, smoke, spoke, stone, stove, wrote	long *o* and long *u* ending in silent *e*
10	brand, bride, crisp, crust, drive, grade, scrape, sprint, stripe, truck	*r* blends
11	branch, crash, fresh, lunch, quench, shelf, shrimp, splash, throne, thumb	consonant digraphs
12	brace, cell, cent, gem, place, price, slice, spice, spruce, stage	soft *c* and soft *g* words
13	blink, bring, chunk, drink, skunk, string, thank, think, trunk, wrong	–*ng* and –*nk* endings
14	away, clay, fray, gray, play, pray, spray, stay, stray, tray	long *a* vowel team *ay*
15	brain, chair, frail, grain, paint, plain, sprain, trail, train, waist	long *a* vowel team *ai*
16	cheap, clean, clear, dream, feast, knead, scream, speak, stream, wreath	long *e* vowel team *ea*
17	bleed, green, kneel, screen, sheet, sleep, speech, street, teeth, three	long *e* vowel team *ee*
18	blind, bright, child, find, flight, fright, grind, knight, mighty, slight	long *i* patterns *igh, ild, ind*
19	boast, coach, coast, croak, float, groan, oath, roast, throat, toast	long *o* vowel team *oa*
20	blow, flow, glow, grow, know, own, slow, snow, stow, throw	long *o* vowel team *ow*

How to Use This Book (cont.)

Unit	Words	Spelling Pattern
21	bolt, both, cold, fold, hold, mold, most, post, sold, told	long *o* patterns *old, olt, ost*
22	bloom, booth, broom, droop, groom, school, scoop, smooth, spoon, tooth	long *u* pattern *oo*
23	blew, crew, drew, fruit, grew, knew, screw, suit, threw, true	long *u* patterns *eu, ew,* and *ui*
24	around, cloud, count, crouch, flour, found, ground, proud, sound, sprout	*ou* diphthong
25	clown, crowd, crown, drown, flower, growl, plow, powder, prowl, scowl	*ow* diphthong
26	broil, cowboy, hoist, joint, moist, ploy, point, spoil, tinfoil, topsoil	*oi/oy* diphthongs
27	broth, cloth, cost, cross, floss, frost, froth, gloss, lost, soft	/ô/ pattern with *o*
28	crawl, draw, fault, flaunt, haul, haunt, scrawl, sprawl, straw, vault	/ô/ pattern with *au* and *aw*
29	also, bald, chalk, scald, stalk, swamp, wand, want, wash, watch	/ô/ pattern with *wa* and *al*
30	brook, bulb, could, crook, gulp, should, skull, stood, sulk, would	schwa sounds
31	can't, didn't, doesn't, I'll, it's, they're, wasn't, we're, who's, you're	contractions
32	carve, charm, march, scarf, shark, sharp, smart, spark, start, starve	*r*-controlled vowels with *ar*
33	four, north, porch, pour, score, short, sport, store, storm, tour	*r*-controlled vowels with *our, or,* and *ore*
34	birth, chirp, first, shirt, squirm, squirt, stir, third, thirst, twirl	*r*-controlled vowels with *ir*
35	blurb, blurt, burst, church, clerk, germs, perch, slurp, stern, were	*r*-controlled vowels with *er* and *ur*
36	candy, funny, happy, jelly, penny, pretty, puppy, silly, twenty, ugly	–*y* endings

Standards Correlations

Shell Education is committed to producing educational materials that are research and standards based. All products are correlated to the academic standards of all 50 states, the District of Columbia, the Department of Defense Dependent Schools, and the Canadian provinces.

How to Find Standards Correlations

To print a customized correlation report of this product for your state, visit **www.tcmpub.com/administrators/correlations/** and follow the online directions. If you require assistance in printing correlation reports, please contact the Customer Service Department at 1-877-777-3450.

Purpose and Intent of Standards

The Every Student Succeeds Act (ESSA) mandates that all states adopt challenging academic standards that help students meet the goal of college and career readiness. While many states already adopted academic standards prior to ESSA, the act continues to hold states accountable for detailed and comprehensive standards.

Standards are designed to focus instruction and guide adoption of curricula. Standards are statements that describe the criteria necessary for students to meet specific academic goals. They define the knowledge, skills, and content students should acquire at each level. Standards are also used to develop standardized tests to evaluate students' academic progress. Teachers are required to demonstrate how their lessons meet state standards. State standards are used in the development of all Shell products, so educators can be assured they meet the academic requirements of each state.

College and Career Readiness

In this book, the following college and career readiness (CCR) standards are met: Generalize learned spelling patterns when writing words; and consult reference materials, including beginning dictionaries, as needed to check and correct spellings.

McREL Compendium

Each year, McREL analyzes state standards and revises the compendium to produce a general compilation of national standards. In this book, the following standards are met: Generalize learned spelling patterns when writing words; and consult reference materials, including beginning dictionaries, as needed to check and correct spellings.

TESOL and WIDA Standards

In this book, the following English language development standards are met: Standard 1: English language learners communicate for social and instructional purposes within the school setting. Standard 2: English language learners communicate information, ideas, and concepts necessary for academic success in the content area of language arts.

UNIT 1
Short A Words

Focus

This week's focus is one-syllable words with short *a* and final blends. Final blends *–sk*, *–st*, *–sp*, and *–ct* are introduced.

Helpful Hint

The *sc* blend shows up at the beginning of a word (*scab, scoop*), but never at the end. Instead, use *–sk* to make the /*sk*/ sound at the end of a word (*mask, task*).

➤ **ask**

➤ **blast**

➤ **cast**

➤ **clasp**

➤ **fact**

➤ **fast**

➤ **last**

➤ **mask**

➤ **past**

➤ **task**

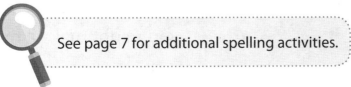

See page 7 for additional spelling activities.

Sentence Completions

Name: _____ **Date:** _____

Directions: Use a word from the Word Bank to complete each sentence.

Word Bank				
ask	blast	cast	clasp	fact
fast	last	mask	past	task

1. I slept at my cousin's house _____ night.

2. A _____ is something I can prove.

3. Miners have to _____ through rock to find coal.

4. My _____ is to shuck all the ears of corn.

5. The doctor put a green _____ on Matt's broken arm.

6. Did you _____ Mom if we could have ice cream?

7. My baby sister cried when I put on my Halloween _____ .

8. The _____ on my necklace is broken.

9. We drove _____ seven For Sale signs on our way to the mall.

10. If you work too _____ , you might make a mistake.

Name: _____ **Date:** _____

Directions: Use a word from the Word Bank for each section.

Synonyms and Antonyms

Word Bank				
ask	blast	cast	clasp	fact
fast	last	mask	past	task

Write a synonym for each word.

1. job _____

2. explode _____

3. truth _____

Write an antonym for each word.

4. slow _____

5. tell _____

6. first _____

7. future _____

Write a word that fits each category.

8. crutches, sling, wheelchair, _____

9. hook, fastener, clip, _____

10. costume, face paint, props, _____

Sentence Types

Name: _____ **Date:** _____

Directions: Study each example. Write a sentence for each word. End each sentence with the same punctuation as the example.

QUESTION   **Ex.**   *close:*   Did you remember to *close* the door?

1. *last:* _____

_____

2. *fast:* _____

_____

STATEMENT   **Ex.**   *note:*   I wrote a thank you *note* to my friend.

3. *fact:* _____

_____

4. *task:* _____

_____

EXCLAMATION   **Ex.**   *bone:*   I found a dinosaur *bone* in my yard!

5. *blast:* _____

_____

6. *mask:* _____

_____

Name: _____ **Date:** _____

Directions: Study how the words change when you add new endings.
Add the same endings to each word to create new words.

1. **bask**   basks   basking   basked

   ask   _____ _____ _____

2. **cast**   casts   casting   casted

   last   _____ _____ _____

3. **rasp**   rasps   rasping   rasped

   clasp _____ _____ _____

Inflectional Endings

Directions: Find three words in the Word Bank that are related to each
of the spelling words. Write the words on the correct lines.

Word Bank				
blasted	faster	blasting	masking	fastest
fastball	unmask	masks	blast off	

4. fast   _____ _____ _____

5. mask   _____ _____ _____

6. blast _____ _____ _____

Name: _____ **Date:** _____

Directions: Use a word from the Word Bank to complete each analogy.

Word Bank				
ask	blast	cast	clasp	fact
fast	last	mask	past	task

1. **body** is to **costume** as **face** is to _____

2. **snail** is to **slow** as **cheetah** is to _____

3. **will walk** is to **future** as **walked** is to _____

4. **belt** is to **buckle** as **necklace** is to _____

5. **sprained wrist** is to **bandage** as **broken wrist** is to _____

6. **oven** is to **heat** as **dynamite** is to _____

7. **drawing** is to **hobby** as **empty the trash** is to _____

8. **engine** is to **first** as **caboose** is to _____

9. **statement** is to **say** as **question** is to _____

10. **"I love milk."** is to **opinion** as **"Milk comes from cows."** is to

_____

UNIT 2
More Short A Words

WEEK 2

➤ **bland**

➤ **damp**

➤ **hand**

➤ **lamp**

➤ **land**

➤ **pants**

➤ **plant**

➤ **slant**

➤ **stamp**

➤ **stand**

Focus

This week's focus is one-syllable words with short *a* and final blends. Final blends *–nd, –mp,* and *–nt* are introduced.

Helpful Hint

Notice that short *a* becomes a nasal sound when it is followed by *m* or *n* (*has, hat, ham, hand*). In this unit, there is a focus on three final blends that contain a nasal short *a*: *–amp, –and, –ant*.

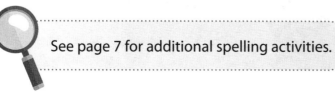

See page 7 for additional spelling activities.

Sentence Completions

Name: _____ **Date:** _____

Directions: Use a word from the Word Bank to complete each sentence.

Word Bank				
bland	damp	hand	lamp	land
pants	plant	slant	stamp	stand

1. Do snails live in the water or on _____ ?

2. It is getting dark. Please turn on the _____ .

3. My dinner was _____ . It needed salt and pepper.

4. Put a _____ on the letter before you mail it.

5. I cut my _____ on the fence.

6. I packed three pairs of _____ and four shirts for the trip.

7. The water slide has a very steep _____ .

8. Please run the dryer again. The towels are still _____ .

9. We had to _____ in line for two hours!

10. Should you _____ tulip bulbs in the fall or spring?

Name: _____ **Date:** _____

Directions: Use a word from the Word Bank for each section.

Synonyms and Antonyms

Word Bank				
bland	damp	hand	lamp	land
pants	plant	slants	stamp	stand

Write a synonym for each word.

1. tilts _____

2. mark _____

3. moist _____

Write an antonym for each word.

4. spicy _____

5. sit down _____

6. dig up _____

7. take off _____

Write a word that fits each category.

8. socks, shirt, hat, _____

9. arm, leg, foot, _____

10. flashlight, candle, light, _____

Sentence Types

Name: _____ **Date:** _____

Directions: Study each example. Write a sentence for each word. End each sentence with the same punctuation as the example.

QUESTION   **Ex.**   *close*:   Did you remember to *close* the door?

1. *plant:* _____

_____

2. *stand*: _____

_____

STATEMENT   **Ex.**   *note*:   I wrote a thank you *note* to my friend.

3. *bland:* _____

_____

4. *lamp:* _____

_____

EXCLAMATION   **Ex.**   *bone*:   I found a dinosaur *bone* in my yard!

5. *pants:* _____

_____

6. *land:* _____

_____

Name: _____ **Date:** _____

Directions: Study how the words change when you add new endings. Add the same endings to each word to create new words.

1. **slant**   slants   slanting   slanted

   plant _____   _____   _____

2. **camp**   camps   camping   camped

   stamp _____   _____   _____

3. **hand**   hands   handing   handed

   land _____   _____   _____

Directions: Find three words in the Word Bank that are related to each of the spelling words. Write the words on the correct lines.

Word Bank				
lampshade	standby	lamps	handshake	handful
standing	kickstand	handy	streetlamp	

4. hand _____   _____   _____

5. stand _____   _____   _____

6. lamp _____   _____   _____

Analogies

Name: _____ **Date:** _____

Directions: Use a word from the Word Bank to complete each analogy.

Word Bank				
bland	damp	hand	lamp	land
pants	plant	slant	stamp	stand

1. **heat** is to **furnace** as **light** is to _____

2. **lake** is to **water** as **island** is to _____

3. **a lot of water** is to **soaked** as **a little water** is to _____

4. **chair** is to **sit** as **floor** is to _____

5. **sock** is to **foot** as **mitten** is to _____

6. **salsa** is to **spicy** as **toast** is to _____

7. **arms** is to **shirt** as **legs** is to _____

8. **fruit** is to **harvest** as **seed** is to _____

9. **passenger** is to **ticket** as **mail** is to _____

10. **C, S, O** is to **curve** as **A, W, X** is to _____

28630—180 Days of Spelling and Word Study © *Shell Education*

UNIT 3
Short I Words

Focus

This week's focus is one-syllable words with short *i* and final blends. Final blends *–ft* and *–lk* are introduced.

Helpful Hint

Notice that the letter *q* never stands alone in English words. It is always followed by the letter *u* (*quilt, squint*).

➤ **gift**

➤ **hint**

➤ **lift**

➤ **list**

➤ **milk**

➤ **mist**

➤ **quilt**

➤ **risk**

➤ **squint**

➤ **twist**

See page 7 for additional spelling activities.

Name: _____ **Date:** _____

Directions: Use a word from the Word Bank to complete each sentence.

Sentence Completions

Word Bank				
gift	hint	lift	list	milk
mist	quilt	risk	squint	twist

1. Let's make a _____ of things to buy at the store.

2. I wrapped Mom's _____ in shiny red paper.

3. A cloud of _____ hung over the lake.

4. If I try to walk in high heels, I will probably _____ my ankle.

5. If you have to _____ to see the page, you might need glasses.

6. Did you add _____ to your bowl of cereal?

7. Some players are too scared to take a _____ , so they don't even swing at the ball.

8. Grammy gave me a new _____ for my bed.

9. You know I don't like surprises. Please give me a

   _____ .

10. Please _____ your feet so I can sweep under the table.

Name: _____ **Date:** _____

Directions: Use a word from the Word Bank for each section.

Word Bank				
gift	hint	lift	list	milk
mist	quilt	risk	squint	twist

Write a synonym for each word.

1. fog _____

2. clue _____

3. present _____

4. take a chance _____

Write an antonym for each word.

5. put down _____

6. open wide _____

7. straighten _____

Write a word that fits each category.

8. sheet, blanket, bedding, _____

9. water, juice, coffee, _____

10. write down, jot down, put in order, _____

Sentence Types

Name: _____ **Date:** _____

Directions: Study each example. Write a sentence for each word. End each sentence with the same punctuation as the example.

QUESTION   **Ex.**   *close*:   Did you remember to *close* the door?

1. *lift:* _____

_____

2. *list*: _____

_____

STATEMENT   **Ex.**   *note*:   I wrote a thank you *note* to my friend.

3. *risk*: _____

_____

4. *squint*: _____

_____

EXCLAMATION   **Ex.**   *bone*:   I found a dinosaur *bone* in my yard!

5. *gift*: _____

_____

6. *milk*: _____

_____

Name: _____ **Date:** _____

Directions: Study how the words change when you add new endings. Add the same endings to each word to create new words.

1. **hint**   hints   hinting   hinted

   squint _____ _____ _____

2. **sift**   sifts   sifting   sifted

   lift _____ _____ _____

3. **list**   lists   listing   listed

   twist _____ _____ _____

Directions: Find three words in the Word Bank that are related to each of the spelling words. Write the words on the correct lines.

Word Bank				
quilts	risky	gifted	gifts	risked
quilting	gift wrap	riskier	quilted	

4. gift _____ _____ _____

5. risk _____ _____ _____

6. quilt _____ _____ _____

Analogies

Name: _____ **Date:** _____

Directions: Use a word from the Word Bank to complete each analogy.

Word Bank				
gift	hint	lift	list	milk
mist	quilt	risk	squint	twist

1. **chicken** is to **eggs** as **cow** is to _____

2. **hearing aid** is to **strain to hear** as **glasses** is to _____

3. **window** is to **curtain** as **bed** is to _____

4. **Halloween** is to **candy** as **birthday** is to _____

5. **foggy** is to **fog** as **misty** is to _____

6. **mystery** is to **clue** as **surprise** is to _____

7. **bulldozer** is to **dig** as **crane** is to _____

8. **asking** is to **ask** as **risking** is to _____

9. **meetings** is to **calendar** as **jobs to do** is to _____

10. **bag of chips** is to **rip open** as **bottle cap** is to _____

28630—180 Days of Spelling and Word Study

© *Shell Education*

UNIT 4
Short E Words

Focus

This week's focus is one-syllable words with short *e* and final blends. Final blends *–lt, –lp, –pt,* and *–xt* are introduced.

Helpful Hint

Sometimes *b* and *d* can be confusing. When students think about *b*, have them think about baseball. Students need a bat first, then the ball. They should draw the stick first, then the curved line to finish the *b*. When students think about *d*, have them think about drums. They should draw the curved line first (the drum), then the stick.

➤ **best**

➤ **blend**

➤ **desk**

➤ **felt**

➤ **help**

➤ **left**

➤ **next**

➤ **slept**

➤ **spend**

➤ **went**

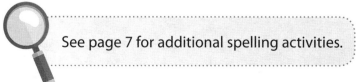

See page 7 for additional spelling activities.

Sentence Completions

Name: _____ **Date:** _____

Directions: Use a word from the Word Bank to complete each sentence.

Word Bank				
best	blend	desk	felt	help
left	next	slept	spend	went

1. We have no school _____ Monday because it's Labor Day.

2. Put all your pencils and books in your _____ .

3. To make a tasty smoothie, _____ yogurt, juice, and fruit together.

4. Can you _____ me tie my shoes?

5. Mrs. Mann is the _____ teacher in the whole world!

6. Dad drove while I _____ in the back seat.

7. We _____ to the store to buy more topsoil.

8. If you _____ all your money on candy, you won't have any left for toys.

9. I _____ so sad for my friend when her dog died.

10. Are there any cookies _____ in the jar?

Name: _____ **Date:** _____

Directions: Use a word from the Word Bank for each section.

Synonyms and Antonyms

Word Bank				
best	blend	desk	felt	help
left	next	slept	spend	went

Write a synonym for each word.

1. mix _____

2. napped _____

3. aid _____

4. touched _____

Write an antonym for each word.

5. came _____

6. worst _____

7. right _____

Write a word that fits each category.

8. first, then, last, _____

9. table, bar, counter, _____

10. use up, buy, purchase, _____

Name: _____ **Date:** _____

Directions: The suffix *–ed* changes a verb to the past tense. Add the suffix *–ed* to each word to change it to the past tense.

Present Tense (Now I...)	Past Tense (Yesterday I...)
rest	
ask	
plant	
twist	
help	

Directions: Some verbs don't follow the *–ed* suffix rule. These words are called *irregular verbs*. Write the past tense of each word.

Present Tense (Now I...)	Past Tense (Yesterday I...)
sleep	
keep	
feel	
leave	
go	

28630—180 Days of Spelling and Word Study
© *Shell Education*

Name: _____ **Date:** _____

Directions: Study how the words change when you add new endings. Add the same endings to each word to create new words.

1. **send**   sends   sending   sent

   spend _____   _____   _____

   bend _____   _____   _____

2. **weep**   weeps   weeping   wept

   sleep _____   _____   _____

   keep _____   _____   _____

Inflectional Endings

Directions: Find three words in the Word Bank that are related to each of the spelling words. Write the words on the correct lines.

Word Bank				
leaving	helping	blender	leave	blended
helpful	blending	helped	leaves	

3. blend _____   _____   _____

4. help _____   _____   _____

5. left _____   _____   _____

Analogies

Name: _____ **Date:** _____

Directions: Use a word from the Word Bank to complete each analogy.

Word Bank				
best	blend	desk	felt	help
left	next	slept	spend	went

1. **dinner** is to **table** as **homework** is to _____

2. **worse** is to **worst** as **better** is to _____

3. **up** is to **down** as **right** is to _____

4. **ingredients** is to **mix** as **colors** is to _____

5. **walk** is to **walked** as **go** is to _____

6. **chair** is to **sat** as **bed** is to _____

7. **toys** is to **play** as **money** is to _____

8. **nose** is to **smelled** as **hands** is to _____

9. **beautiful** is to **beauty** as **helpful** is to _____

10. **test** is to **nest** as **text** is to _____

© Shell Education

UNIT 5
Short O and Short U Words

➤ **blunt**

➤ **does**

➤ **dusk**

➤ **fond**

➤ **jump**

➤ **just**

➤ **must**

➤ **pond**

➤ **stomp**

➤ **stump**

Focus

This week's focus is one-syllable words with short *o* or short *u* and final blends.

Helpful Hint

The word *does* is a rule breaker. Its spelling doesn't make sense, so students will need to create their own tricks for visualizing and spelling it correctly.

See page 7 for additional spelling activities.

Sentence Completions

Name: _____ **Date:** _____

Directions: Use a word from the Word Bank to complete each sentence.

Word Bank				
blunt	does	dusk	fond	jump
just	must	pond	stomp	stump

1. I can only reach the top shelf if I _____ .

2. We watched the sun go down at _____ .

3. Grandma has _____ memories of her childhood in Kansas.

4. My parents make rules that are fair and _____ .

5. Have you ever gone swimming in the _____ ?

6. Let's put on boots and _____ our feet in puddles!

7. Mom says I _____ brush my teeth at least twice a day.

8. Little kids have to use _____ scissors so they don't cut themselves.

9. After Dad chopped down the tree, I helped him dig up the

    _____ .

10. What _____ an owl sound like?

Name: _____ **Date:** _____

Directions: Use a word from the Word Bank for each section.

Word Bank				
blunt	does	dusk	fond	jump
just	must	pond	stomp	stump

Write a synonym for each word.

1. loving _____

2. have to _____

3. fair _____

4. small lake _____

Write an antonym for each word.

5. sharp _____

6. tiptoe _____

7. dawn _____

Write a word that fits each category.

8. skip, hop, leap, _____

9. branch, limb, trunk, _____

10. did, didn't, doesn't, _____

Sentence Types

Name: _____ **Date:** _____

Directions: Study each example. Write a sentence for each word. End each sentence with the same punctuation as the example.

QUESTION   **Ex.**   *close*:   Did you remember to *close* the door?

1. *jump*: _____

_____

2. *pond*: _____

_____

STATEMENT   **Ex.**   *note*:   I wrote a thank you *note* to my friend.

3. *blunt*: _____

_____

4. *dusk*: _____

_____

EXCLAMATION   **Ex.**   *bone*:   I found a dinosaur *bone* in my yard!

5. *must*: _____

_____

6. *stomp*: _____

_____

Name: _____ **Date:** _____

Directions: Sort the words in the Word Bank into two categories: *Present Tense Verbs* and *Past Tense Verbs*. Write each word in the correct column.

Word Bank				
jumped	dump	dusted	rust	pump
stomped	hunted	bunt	stop	bumped

Present Tense Verbs	Past Tense Verbs
○	○
○	○
○	○
○	○
○	○

Directions: Write all 10 words in ABC order.

1. _____   6. _____

2. _____   7. _____

3. _____   8. _____

4. _____   9. _____

5. _____   10. _____

Name: _____ **Date:** _____

Directions: Use a word from the Word Bank to complete each analogy.

Analogies

Word Bank				
blunt	does	dusk	fond	jump
just	must	pond	stomp	stump

1. **morning** is to **dawn** as **evening** is to _____

2. **river** is to **stream** as **lake** is to _____

3. **soldier** is to **brave** as **judge** is to _____

4. **kindness** is to **kind** as **fondness** is to _____

5. **dig up tree** is to **hole** as **cut down tree** is to _____

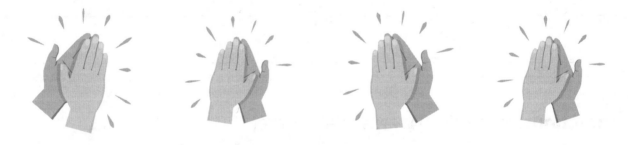

6. **hands** is to **clap** as **feet** is to _____

7. **new pencil** is to **sharp** as **old pencil** is to _____

8. **am** is to **is** as **do** is to _____

9. **jungle gym** is to **climb** as **trampoline** is to _____

10. **might** is to **will** as **can** is to _____

UNIT 6
–ck Ending

Focus

This week's focus is one-syllable words that start with a blend and end with a short vowel plus –ck.

Helpful Hint

The –ck ending only follows a single vowel that makes a short vowel sound (ack, eck, ick, ock, uck). It also only appears at the end of a word or syllable.

- black
- click
- clock
- flock
- pluck
- smock
- snack
- speck
- stack
- stick

See page 7 for additional spelling activities.

Sentence Completions

Name: _____ Date:_____

Directions: Use a word from the Word Bank to complete each sentence.

Word Bank				
black	click	clock	flock	pluck
smock	snack	speck	stack	stick

1. Wear your _____ when you paint so you don't ruin your clothes.

2. Dad left a _____ of mail on the kitchen table.

3. Some people use tweezers to _____ splinters from fingers.

4. There's not even a _____ of dirt on Nana's floor.

5. I am not afraid of _____ cats.

6. Please look at the _____ and tell me what time it is.

7. If you _____ on the wrong button, you will end up at a different website.

8. I always get a _____ when I get home from school.

9. There was a whole _____ of turkeys standing in my driveway yesterday!

10. My poster keeps falling off the wall because the tape doesn't

    _____ anymore.

Name: _____ **Date:**_____

Directions: Use a word from the Word Bank for each section.

Word Bank				
black	click	clock	flock	pluck
smock	snack	speck	stack	stick

Write a synonym for each word.

1. pile _____

2. apron _____

3. pull _____

Write an antonym for each word.

4. white _____

5. come apart _____

6. meal _____

7. large stain _____

Write a word that fits each category.

8. herd, colony, pack, _____

9. push, press, select, _____

10. watch, sundial, hourglass, _____

Prefixes and Suffixes

Name: _____ Date: _____

Directions: Complete the chart by adding *–ing* and *–ed* to the words.

Verb	Add *–ing*	Add *–ed*
click		
snack		
pick		
stack		
block		

Directions: Use a word from the chart to fill in each blank.

1. I was _____ dirty dishes in the sink when the doorbell rang.

2. I _____ two more books for my reading bag.

3. I can't open the door. A pile of boxes is _____ it.

4. We _____ on orange slices during halftime.

5. Isabella _____ the Save button before she shut off her computer.

Name: _____ **Date:** _____

Directions: Study how the words change when you add new endings. Add the same endings to each word to create new words.

1. **flick**   flicks   flicking   flicked

   click _____ _____ _____

2. **pack**   packs   packing   packed

   stack _____ _____ _____

3. **cluck**   clucks   clucking   clucked

   pluck _____ _____ _____

Inflectional Endings

Directions: Find three words in the Word Bank that are related to each of the spelling words. Write the words on the correct lines.

Word Bank				
clockwise	blacksmith	blacken	clocks	stuck
sticky	sticking	clockwork	blackest	

4. stick _____ _____ _____

5. black _____ _____ _____

6. clock _____ _____ _____

Analogies

Name: _____ Date: _____

Directions: Use a word from the Word Bank to complete each analogy.

Word Bank				
black	click	clock	flock	pluck
smock	snack	speck	stack	stick

1. **day sky** is to **blue** as **night sky** is to _____

2. **scissors** is to **cut** as **glue** is to _____

3. **sheep** is to **herd** as **birds** is to _____

4. **leaves** is to **pile** as **firewood** is to _____

5. **keyboard** is to **type** as **mouse** is to _____

6. **food** is to **crumb** as **dust** is to _____

7. **cooking** is to **apron** as **art projects** is to _____

8. **hairs** is to **shave** as **feathers** is to _____

9. **wrist** is to **watch** as **wall** is to _____

10. **bacon and eggs** is to **breakfast** as **apple slices** is to

_____

UNIT 7
Silent Letters

Focus

This week's focus is one-syllable words that start or end with a silent letter. The *–mb, kn–,* and *wr–* patterns are introduced.

Helpful Hint

Notice that silent letters always hang out with a buddy. For example, silent *k* only comes before *n (knit, knob)*. Silent *b* only comes after *m (lamb, numb)*. Silent *w* only comes before *r (wrap, wrist)*. Practice silent letters in pairs, not on their own.

- ➤ **knelt**
- ➤ **knit**
- ➤ **knob**
- ➤ **knock**
- ➤ **knot**
- ➤ **lamb**
- ➤ **numb**
- ➤ **wrap**
- ➤ **wreck**
- ➤ **wrist**

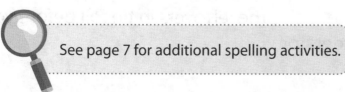

See page 7 for additional spelling activities.

Name: _____ **Date:** _____

Directions: Use a word from the Word Bank to complete each sentence.

Word Bank				
knelt	knit	knob	knock	knot
lamb	numb	wrap	wreck	wrist

Sentence Completions

1. My lips and cheek felt _____ for an hour after I got my cavity filled.

2. I have a _____ hat and scarf for cold days.

3. They're going to _____ down the old factory and build a shopping mall.

4. I can't tie my shoelaces because there's a giant _____ in one of them.

5. The sheep next door just birthed a _____ .

6. I _____ down in the front row when we took a team picture.

7. Why did you _____ my tower of blocks?

8. I can't open the drawer because the _____ fell off.

9. My stepmom likes to wear lots of colorful bracelets around her

   _____ .

10. Please _____ the leftovers in tin foil before you put them in the refrigerator.

Name: _____ **Date:** _____

Directions: Use a word from the Word Bank for each section.

Word Bank				
knelt	knit	knob	knock	knot
lamb	numb	wrap	wreck	wrist

Write a synonym for each word.

1. sheep _____

2. bang _____

3. handle _____

4. unfeeling _____

Write an antonym for each word.

5. fix _____

6. uncover _____

7. stood up _____

Write a word that fits each category.

8. elbow, ankle, knee, _____

9. sew, weave, embroider, _____

10. tie, bow, loop, _____

Sentence Types

Name: _____ **Date:** _____

Directions: Study each example. Write a sentence for each word. End each sentence with the same punctuation as the example.

QUESTION   **Ex.**   *close*:   Did you remember to *close* the door?

1. *numb*: _____

_____

2. *wrap*: _____

_____

STATEMENT   **Ex.**   *note*:   I wrote a thank you *note* to my friend.

3. *wrist*: _____

_____

4. *knot*: _____

_____

EXCLAMATION   **Ex.**   *bone*:   I found a dinosaur *bone* in my yard!

5. *wreck*: _____

_____

6. *knock*: _____

_____

Name: _____ **Date:** _____

Directions: Study how the words change when you add new endings. Add the same endings to each word to create new words.

1. **feel**   feels   feeling   felt

   kneel _____ _____ _____

2. **pot**   pots   potting   potted

   knot _____ _____ _____

3. **peck**   pecks   pecking   pecked

   wreck _____ _____ _____

Directions: Find three words in the Word Bank that are related to each of the spelling words. Write the words on the correct lines.

Word Bank				
unwrap	doorknob	knitting	knobby	knitter
wrapper	wrapping	knits	knobs	

4. wrap _____ _____ _____

5. knit _____ _____ _____

6. knob _____ _____ _____

Analogies

Name: _____ **Date:** _____

Directions: Use a word from the Word Bank to complete each analogy.

Word Bank				
knelt	knit	knob	knock	knot
lamb	numb	wrap	wreck	wrist

1. **doorbell** is to **ring** as **door** is to _____

2. **feel** is to **felt** as **kneel** is to _____

3. **foot** is to **ankle** as **hand** is to _____

4. **cow** is to **calf** as **sheep** is to _____

5. **letter** is to **envelope** as **present** is to _____

6. **thread** is to **sew** as **yarn** is to _____

7. **trip** is to **fall** as **accident** is to _____

8. **refrigerator door** is to **handle** as **front door** is to _____

9. **hair** is to **tangle** as **rope** is to _____

10. **very hot hands** is to **sweaty** as **very cold hands** is to

_____

UNIT 8
Long A and Long I Words Ending in Silent E

WEEK 8

Focus

This week's focus is one-syllable words with beginning blends, long *a* or long *i*, and silent *e*.

Helpful Hint

All words on this list are considered *"bossy e"* words because the *e* at the end of the word jumps over the consonant and orders the vowel to say its name.

- ➤ **flake**
- ➤ **knife**
- ➤ **plate**
- ➤ **skate**
- ➤ **slide**
- ➤ **smile**
- ➤ **snake**
- ➤ **stale**
- ➤ **state**
- ➤ **write**

See page 7 for additional spelling activities.

Sentence Completions

Name: _____ **Date:** _____

Directions: Use a word from the Word Bank to complete each sentence.

Word Bank				
flake	knife	plate	skate	slide
smile	snake	stale	state	write

1. Please put your toast on a _____ so you don't get crumbs everywhere.

2. Remember to _____ a thank you note to Grandpa!

3. My baby sister sat on my lap when we went down the

   _____ .

4. The old paint began to _____ off the wall.

5. Bread will get _____ faster if you forget to close the bag.

6. My friend Trenton feeds frozen mice to his pet _____ .

7. If it gets cold enough, we might be able to _____ on the pond this winter.

8. My best friend moved to another _____ , but we still text each other all the time.

9. You need a sharp _____ to cut open the pineapple.

10. Mom had a big _____ on her face when I walked in the door.

28630—180 Days of Spelling and Word Study

Name: _____ **Date:**_____

Directions: Use a word from the Word Bank for each section.

Word Bank				
flake	knife	plate	skate	slide
smile	snake	stale	state	write

Write a synonym for each word.

1. dish _____

2. blade _____

3. small,
flat piece _____

Write an antonym for each word.

4. frown _____

5. fresh _____

6. erase _____

7. ladder _____

Write a word that fits each category.

8. alligator, turtle, lizard, _____

9. town, country, continent, _____

10. ski, sled, snowboard, _____

Verb Tenses

Name: _____ **Date:** _____

Directions: Add an *–ing* and *–ed* suffix to each word. Remember to drop the bossy *e* first.

Verb	Add *–ing*	Add *–ed*
skate		
flake		
smile		
state		
blame		

Directions: Some verbs don't follow the *–ed* suffix rule. These words are called *irregular verbs*. Write the past tense of each irregular verb.

Present Tense (Now I…)	Past Tense (Yesterday I…)
slide	
write	
take	
make	
bite	

Name: _____ **Date:**_____

Directions: Study how the words change when you add new endings. Add the same endings to each word to create new words.

1. **hate** hates hating hated

   skate _____ _____ _____

2. **file** files filing filed

   smile _____ _____ _____

3. **rake** rakes raking raked

   flake _____ _____ _____

Directions: Find three words in the Word Bank that are related to each of the spelling words. Write the words on the correct lines.

Word Bank				
snakeskin	wrote	rattlesnake	sliding	slid
slides	snakes	writer	writing	

4. write _____ _____ _____

5. slide _____ _____ _____

6. snake _____ _____ _____

Analogies

Name: _____ **Date:** _____

Directions: Use a word from the Word Bank to complete each analogy.

Word Bank				
flake	knife	plate	skate	slide
smile	snake	stale	state	write

1. **up** is to **ladder** as **down** is to _____

2. **mammal** is to **whale** as **reptile** is to _____

3. **meat** is to **spoiled** as **bread** is to _____

4. **United States** is to **country** as **Maryland** is to _____

5. **scoop** is to **spoon** as **cut** is to _____

6. **rain** is to **drop** as **snow** is to _____

7. **unhappy** is to **frown** as **happy** is to _____

8. **floor** is to **dance** as **ice** is to _____

9. **eraser** is to **erase** as **pencil** is to _____

10. **ice cream** is to **bowl** as **cake** is to _____

28630—180 Days of Spelling and Word Study   © *Shell Education*

UNIT 9
Long O and Long U Words Ending in Silent E

Focus

This week's focus is one-syllable words with beginning blends, long *o* or long *u*, and silent *e*.

Helpful Hint

All of the words on this list are considered *"bossy e"* words. Sometimes, bossy *e* has more than one job. In some cases, it changes the sound of the consonant that comes right before it. For example, bossy *e* can make *s* sound like /z/ in words like *close* and *please*.

- close
- flute
- globe
- plume
- slope
- smoke
- spoke
- stone
- stove
- wrote

See page 7 for additional spelling activities.

Sentence Completions

Name: _____ **Date:**_____

Directions: Use a word from the Word Bank to complete each sentence.

Word Bank				
close	flute	globe	plume	slope
smoke	spoke	stone	stove	wrote

1. Mom _____ to the doctor about my fever.

2. Let's _____ the windows so the rain doesn't come in.

3. Can you find China on the _____ ?

4. I _____ a story about aliens in class today.

5. There's more soup on the _____ if you're hungry.

6. My sister started playing the _____ when she was in fourth grade.

7. Dad made a Peter Pan costume and sewed a red

   _____ to my hat.

8. The _____ in our front yard is great for sledding.

9. I stepped away from the campfire because the _____ kept blowing in my eyes.

10. I helped my mom build a _____ walkway up to the front door.

Name: _____ **Date:** _____

Directions: Use a word from the Word Bank for each section.

Word Bank				
close	flute	globe	plume	slope
smoke	spoke	stone	stove	wrote

Write a synonym for each word.

1. sphere _____

2. oven _____

3. slant _____

4. feather _____

Write an antonym for each word.

5. open _____

6. listened _____

7. erased _____

Write a word that fits each category.

8. oboe, clarinet, saxophone, _____

9. steam, smog, fog, _____

10. pebble, rock, boulder, _____

Verb Tenses

Name: _____ **Date:** _____

Directions: Add an *–ing* and *–ed* suffix to each word. Remember to drop the bossy *e* first.

Verb	Add *–ing*	Add *–ed*
smoke		
slope		
hope		
vote		
close		

Directions: Some verbs don't follow the *–ed* suffix rule. These words are called *irregular verbs*. Write the past tense of each irregular verb.

Present Tense (Now I…)	Past Tense (Yesterday I…)
speak	
steal	
write	
freeze	
wake	

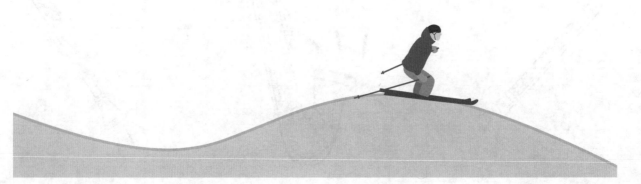

28630—180 Days of Spelling and Word Study
© Shell Education

Name: _____ **Date:** _____

Directions: Answer each question in a complete sentence. Turn the question around, and use the bold word in each answer.

1. Why do some kids play the **flute**?

   _____

   _____

2. Why do people look at a **globe**?

   _____

   _____

3. Why is it important to **close** the freezer door tightly?

   _____

   _____

4. What can you cook on the **stove**?

   _____

   _____

5. Why are **smoke** alarms placed on the ceiling?

   _____

   _____

6. What can people make out of **stone**?

   _____

   _____

Analogies

Name: _____ **Date:** _____

Directions: Use a word from the Word Bank to complete each analogy.

Word Bank				
close	flute	globe	plume	slope
smoke	spoke	stone	stove	wrote

1. **percussion** is to **drum** as **woodwind** is to _____

2. **car** is to **exhaust** as **fire** is to _____

3. **porcupine** is to **quill** as **peacock** is to _____

4. **two-dimensional** is to **map** as **three-dimensional** is to

   _____

5. **wash** is to **sink** as **cook** is to _____

6. **cross country ski** is to **flat land** as **downhill ski** is to

   _____

7. **listener** is to **listened** as **speaker** is to _____

8. **pull** is to **open** as **push** is to _____

9. **fence** is to **wood** as **wall** is to _____

10. **keyboard** is to **typed** as **pen** is to _____

Unit 10
R Blends

Focus

This week's focus is one-syllable words with beginning *r* blends followed by a long vowel and silent *e* or a short vowel and final blend.

Helpful Hint

R blends can be tricky. Students often hear a */j/* sound at the beginning of words such as *drink* and *drip*, so make sure to accentuate the */d/* sound when spelling them. Also, make sure students always pronounce *r* as */r/*, not */er/*. This will help them avoid common spelling mistakes as well.

- brand
- bride
- crisp
- crust
- drive
- grade
- scrape
- sprint
- stripe
- truck

See page 7 for additional spelling activities.

Sentence Completions

Name: _____ **Date:** _____

Directions: Use a word from the Word Bank to complete each sentence.

Word Bank				
brand	bride	crisp	crust	drive
grade	scrape	sprint	stripe	truck

1. Keep toasting the bread until it's nice and _____ .

2. I am happy with the _____ I earned on my test.

3. Can you fit all this furniture in the back of your

   _____ ?

4. Skunks have a long, white _____ on their back.

5. Sasha, can you _____ me to the mall today?

6. Which _____ of markers is your favorite?

7. I think the _____ is the best part of an apple pie.

8. We had to _____ ice off the windshield before we could drive anywhere.

9. Doesn't the _____ look beautiful in her long, white gown?

10. I tried to _____ to the finish line, but I was too exhausted.

Name: _____ **Date:** _____

Directions: Use a word from the Word Bank for each section.

Word Bank				
brand	bride	crisp	crust	drive
grade	scrape	sprint	stripe	truck

Write a synonym for each word.

1. scratch _____

2. score _____

3. steer _____

4. coating _____

Write an antonym for each word.

5. groom _____

6. mush _____

7. walk _____

Write a word that fits each category.

8. bike, car, bus, _____

9. zigzag, polka dot, checker, _____

10. stand, grand, bland, _____

Synonyms and Antonyms

Word Sorts

Name: _____ **Date:** _____

Directions: Sort the words in the Word Bank into two categories: *Short Vowel Words* and *Long Vowel Words.* Write each word in the correct column.

Word Bank				
grade	stripe	truck	sprint	scrape
brand	drive	crust	bride	crisp

Short Vowel Words	Long Vowel Words
○	○
○	○
○	○
○	○
○	○

Directions: Write all 10 words in ABC order.

1. _____

2. _____

3. _____

4. _____

5. _____

6. _____

7. _____

8. _____

9. _____

10. _____

Name: _____ **Date:** _____

Directions: Study how the words change when you add new endings. Add the same endings to each word to create new words.

1. **trade**   trades   trading   traded

   grade _____   _____   _____

2. **hint**   hints   hinting   hinted

   sprint _____   _____   _____

3. **shape**   shapes   shaping   shaped

   scrape _____   _____   _____

Directions: Find three words in the Word Bank that are related to each of the spelling words. Write the words on the correct lines.

Word Bank				
driver	trucks	crispy	drove	driving
truckload	crispier	crispiest	trucker	

4. drive _____   _____   _____

5. crisp _____   _____   _____

6. truck _____   _____   _____

Analogies

Name: _____ **Date:** _____

Directions: Use a word from the Word Bank to complete each analogy.

Word Bank				
brand	bride	crisp	crust	drive
grade	scrape	sprint	stripe	truck

1. **cake** is to **frosting** as **pie** is to _____

2. **seven** is to **age** as **second** is to _____

3. **bike** is to **ride** as **car** is to _____

4. **husband** is to **wife** as **groom** is to _____

5. **oatmeal** is to **mush** as **crackers** is to _____

6. **slow** is to **jog** as **fast** is to _____

7. **police** is to **car** as **fire** is to _____

8. **round** is to **polka dot** as **straight** is to _____

9. **team** is to **team name** as **company** is to _____

10. **dirt** is to **scrub** as **dried gum** is to _____

UNIT 11
Consonant Digraphs

➤ **branch**

➤ **crash**

➤ **fresh**

➤ **lunch**

➤ **quench**

➤ **shelf**

➤ **shrimp**

➤ **splash**

➤ **throne**

➤ **thumb**

Focus

This week's focus is one-syllable words that contain consonant digraphs (*ch, sh, th*) at the beginning or end of the word.

Helpful Hint

This is the first time students have practiced consonant digraph blends such as *shr* and *thr* (*shrimp, throne*). Help them stretch out each sound by tapping it on their fingers or on the tabletop: *sh-r-i-m-p*. Students might also need help listening for the /n/ sound in words such as *branch* and *lunch*. Tap this word out too: *l-u-n-ch*. Notice that consonant digraphs (*ch, sh, th*) are never pulled apart.

🔍 See page 7 for additional spelling activities.

Sentence Completions

Name: _____ Date: _____

Directions: Use a word from the Word Bank to complete each sentence.

Word Bank				
branch	crash	fresh	lunch	quench
shelf	shrimp	splash	throne	thumb

1. When I jumped off the diving board, I made a big

   _____ in the water.

2. We hung our tire swing from a _____ of the oak tree.

3. I got a blister on my _____ when I climbed up
   the rope.

4. Put the soup on the top _____ of the pantry.

5. We are going outside for recess after _____ .

6. This cold glass of ice water will _____ your thirst!

7. You will find _____ on the menu at most seafood
   restaurants.

8. Strawberries taste so _____ and delicious when
   you pick them yourself!

9. The king sat on his _____ and gave orders to
   his knights.

10. If you pile too many heavy books on the shelf, it will

    _____ to the floor.

Name: _____ **Date:** _____

Directions: Use a word from the Word Bank for each section.

Word Bank				
branch	crash	fresh	lunch	quench
shelf	shrimp	splash	throne	thumb

Write a synonym for each word.

1. splatter _____

2. tree limb _____

3. ledge _____

4. midday meal_____

Write an antonym for each word.

5. stale _____

6. be thirsty _____

7. swerve _____

Write a word that fits each category.

8. chair, stool, seat, _____

9. clams, lobster, scallops, _____

10. pinkie, ring finger, middle finger, _____

Name: _____ **Date:** _____

Directions: *Plural* means more than one. If a word ends with *ch* or *sh*, add *–es* to the word to make it plural. Add *–es* to each word.

Prefixes and Suffixes

Singular Noun	Plural Noun (Add *–es*)
bench	
brush	
lunch	
flash	
punch	

Directions: Change each word to a plural noun.

Singular Noun	Plural Noun (Change the *f* to *v* and add *–es*)
shelf	
elf	
half	
calf	
wife	

When a word ends with the */f/* sound, make it plural by changing the *f* to a *v* and adding *–es*.

Name: _____ **Date:**_____

Directions: Study how the words change when you add new endings. Add the same endings to each word to create new words.

1. **mash**   mashes   mashing   mashed

     splash _____ _____ _____

2. **munch**   munches   munching   munched

     crunch _____ _____ _____

3. **drench**   drenches   drenching   drenched

     quench _____ _____ _____

Directions: Find three words in the Word Bank that are related to each of the spelling words. Write the words on the correct lines.

Word Bank				
fresher	lunches	thumbtack	thumbnail	freshly
lunchroom	thumbs	lunchtime	freshness	

4. thumb _____ _____ _____

5. lunch _____ _____ _____

6. fresh _____ _____ _____

Inflectional Endings

Name: _____ **Date:** _____

Directions: Use a word from the Word Bank to complete each analogy.

Word Bank				
branch	crash	fresh	lunch	quench
shelf	shrimp	splash	throne	thumb

1. **hot oil** is to **splatter** as **swimming pool** is to _____

2. **foot** is to **big toe** as **hand** is to _____

3. **person** is to **arm** as **tree** is to _____

4. **baby** is to **high chair** as **king** is to _____

5. **land** is to **scorpion** as **water** is to _____

6. **pancakes** is to **breakfast** as **sandwich** is to _____

7. **dresser** is to **drawer** as **closet** is to _____

8. **ship** is to **wreck** as **plane** is to _____

9. **snack** is to **satisfy** as **drink** is to _____

10. **picked last month** is to **rotten** as **picked today** is to

_____

UNIT 12
Soft C and Soft G Words

- brace
- cell
- cent
- gem
- place
- price
- slice
- spice
- spruce
- stage

Focus

This week's focus is one-syllable words that start with soft *c* or soft *g* or start with a beginning blend and end with soft *c* or soft *g*.

Helpful Hint

Remember that bossy *e* has more than one job. Besides making a vowel say its name, it changes the sound of *c* or *g* when they appear right before the bossy *e*. The *c* becomes soft (*spice*) and the *g* becomes soft (*stage*). *C* and *g* are usually soft when they appear before *e, i,* or *y*.

See page 7 for additional spelling activities.

Sentence Completions

Name: _____ Date: _____

Directions: Use a word from the Word Bank to complete each sentence.

Word Bank				
brace	cell	cent	gem	place
price	slice	spice	spruce	stage

1. The _____ of gas keeps going up. It's almost $3 per gallon!

2. We will _____ up the bedroom with fresh paint.

3. Reggie has to wear a _____ on his knee every time he runs.

4. The inmate is allowed to leave his _____ for two hours a day.

5. Cape Cod is my favorite _____ in the whole world!

6. I would like one _____ of that tasty banana bread.

7. My grandma said she could buy candy for one _____ when she was little.

8. A diamond is a precious _____ .

9. I stood on _____ and recited my poem to the whole school.

10. There's too much _____ in this chili. It's burning my mouth!

28630—180 Days of Spelling and Word Study

Name: _____ **Date:** _____

Directions: Sort the words in the Word Bank into two categories: *Short Vowel Words* and *Long Vowel Words*. Write each word in the correct column.

Word Bank				
since	price	gem	place	cent
cell	stage	spice	gel	slice

Short Vowel Words	Long Vowel Words
○	○
○	○
○	○
○	○
○	○

Directions: Write all 10 words in ABC order.

1. _____   6. _____

2. _____   7. _____

3. _____   8. _____

4. _____   9. _____

5. _____   10. _____

Name: _____ **Date:**_____

Directions: Answer each question in a complete sentence. Turn the question around, and use the bold word in each answer.

1. Why do some people get nervous on **stage**?

   _____

   _____

2. What can you do to **spruce** up your bedroom?

   _____

   _____

3. Why do people add **spices** to their cooking?

   _____

   _____

4. What is your favorite kind of **gem**?

   _____

   _____

5. Why should you **place** your homework in your backpack before bed?

   _____

   _____

6. Why do some people need **braces** for their teeth?

   _____

   _____

Name: _____ Date:_____

Directions: Study how the words change when you add new endings. Add the same endings to each word to create new words.

1. **dice**   dices   dicing   diced

   slice _____ _____ _____

2. **race**   races   racing   raced

   place _____ _____ _____

3. **rage**   rages   raging   raged

   stage _____ _____ _____

Directions: Find three words in the Word Bank that are related to each of the spelling words. Write the words on the correct lines.

Word Bank				
spicy	cells	priceless	cellular	pricey
overpriced	spices	spiced	cell phone	

4. spice _____ _____ _____

5. price _____ _____ _____

6. cell _____ _____ _____

Analogies

Name: _____ **Date:** _____

Directions: Use a word from the Word Bank to complete each analogy.

Word Bank				
brace	cell	cent	gem	place
price	slice	spice	spruce	stage

1. **broken** is to **cast** as **sprained** is to _____

2. **sugar** is to **sweetener** as **pepper** is to _____

3. **$** is to **dollar** as **¢** is to _____

4. **movie** is to **screen** as **play** is to _____

5. **Santa Claus** is to **person** as **North Pole** is to _____

6. **bird** is to **cage** as **prisoner** is to _____

7. **gold** is to **metal** as **diamond** is to _____

8. **butter** is to **pat** as **bread** is to _____

9. **large** is to **size** as **$29.99** is to _____

10. **scrub the floor** is to **clean** as **paint the walls** is to

    _____

UNIT 13
–ng and –nk Endings

- blink
- bring
- chunk
- drink
- skunk
- string
- thank
- think
- trunk
- wrong

Focus

This week's focus is one-syllable words that start with a consonant blend or digraph and end with –ng or –nk.

Helpful Hint

When spelling –nk words such as *blink*, encourage students to tap out each sound first: *b-l-i-n-k.* This will help them avoid the common mistake of adding an *ng* before the *k* sound *(blingk)*.

See page 7 for additional spelling activities.

Sentence Completions

Name: _____ **Date:** _____

Directions: Use a word from the Word Bank to complete each sentence.

Word Bank				
blink	bring	chunk	drink	skunk
string	thank	think	trunk	wrong

1. Stay away from that _____ or it might get scared and spray you.

2. When my eyes feel dry, I start to _____ a lot.

3. May I have a _____ of water? I'm so thirsty!

4. There is a spare tire in the _____ of the car.

5. I let go of the balloon's _____ and it floated away.

6. Remember to say _____ you when someone gives you a gift.

7. If you take a _____ turn, you will probably get lost.

8. Will you _____ me a present when you come back from your trip?

9. A big _____ of rock rolled off the cliff.

10. Do you _____ we will ever be able to send a person to Mars?

Name: _____ **Date:** _____

Directions: Use a word from the Word Bank for each section.

Synonyms and Antonyms

Word Bank				
blink	bring	chunk	drink	skunk
string	thank	think	trunk	wrong

Write a synonym for each word.

1. glob _____

2. sip _____

3. ponder _____

4. wink _____

Write an antonym for each word.

5. right _____

6. hood _____

7. take away _____

Write a word that fits each category.

8. thread, yarn, ribbon, _____

9. beaver, porcupine, mole, _____

10. please, you're welcome, excuse me, _____

Name: _____ **Date:**_____

Directions: Study how the words change when you add new endings. Add the same endings to each word to create new words.

1. **sink** sinks sinking sank

   drink _____ _____ _____

2. **wink** winks winking winked

   blink _____ _____ _____

3. **rank** ranks ranking ranked

   thank _____ _____ _____

Directions: Find three words in the Word Bank that are related to each of the spelling words. Write the words on the correct lines.

Word Bank				
drawstring	brings	thinks	stringy	thinking
bringing	strings	brought	thought	

4. bring _____ _____ _____

5. think _____ _____ _____

6. string _____ _____ _____

Name: _____ **Date:** _____

Directions: The suffix *–ed* changes a verb (an action word) to the past tense. Add the suffix *–ed* to each verb to change it to the past tense.

Present Tense (Now I…)	Past Tense (Yesterday I…)
thank	
blink	
bang	
dunk	
honk	

Directions: Some verbs don't follow the *–ed* suffix rule. These words are called *irregular verbs*. Write the past tense of each verb.

Present Tense (Now I…)	Past Tense (Yesterday I…)
think	
bring	
drink	
sing	
sink	

Verb Tenses

Analogies

Name: _____ **Date:** _____

Directions: Use a word from the Word Bank to complete each analogy.

Word Bank				
blink	bring	chunk	drink	skunk
string	thank	think	trunk	wrong

1. **spots** is to **cheetah** as **stripe** is to _____

2. **piano** is to **key** as **guitar** is to _____

3. **heart** is to **feel** as **brain** is to _____

4. **bird** is to **beak** as **elephant** is to _____

5. **apple** is to **food** as **juice** is to _____

6. **3 + 3 = 6** is to **right** as **3 + 3 = 7** is to _____

7. **runt** is to **blunt** as **wink** is to _____

8. **thought** is to **think** as **brought** is to _____

9. **handshake** is to **greet** as **hug** is to _____

10. **mint chip ice cream** is to **chip** as **cookie dough ice cream** is to

_____

28630—180 Days of Spelling and Word Study   © *Shell Education*

UNIT 14
Long A Vowel Team *ay*

➤ **away**

➤ **clay**

➤ **fray**

➤ **gray**

➤ **play**

➤ **pray**

➤ **spray**

➤ **stay**

➤ **stray**

➤ **tray**

Focus

This week's focus is one-syllable words that start with a consonant blend and end with *ay*.

Helpful Hint

Notice that the *ay* pattern is only used at the end of a base word (*tray*) or syllable (*cray·on, play·er*), never in the middle. When adding suffixes to *ay* words, keep the base word the same (*play—playing, spray—sprayed*).

See page 7 for additional spelling activities.

Name: _____ **Date:** _____

Directions: Use a word from the Word Bank to complete each sentence.

Sentence Completions

Word Bank				
away	clay	fray	gray	play
pray	spray	stay	stray	tray

1. Don't _____ from the path, or you might get lost in the woods.

2. We put Mom's breakfast on a _____ and delivered it to her in bed.

3. I was very sad when my best friend moved _____ last summer.

4. The sky always looks _____ on rainy days.

5. We have to buy a new leash for the dog. This one is starting to

   _____ .

6. We're making _____ pots in art class next week!

7. The _____ from the sprinklers got my mom's car wet.

8. Are you going to rent a house or _____ in a hotel when you go on vacation?

9. Some families _____ when they sit down to eat a meal together.

10. I might _____ soccer in the fall.

Name: _____ **Date:** _____

Directions: Use a word from the Word Bank for each section.

Word Bank				
away	clay	fray	gray	play
pray	spray	stay	stray	tray

Write a synonym for each word.

1. unravel _____

2. wander off _____

3. ask for _____

Write an antonym for each word.

4. toward _____

5. fight _____

6. leave _____

Write a word that fits each category.

7. black, white, tan, _____

8. squirt, shoot, sprinkle, _____

9. pizza dough, cookie dough, play dough, _____

10. platter, serving dish, cutting board, _____

Inflectional Endings

Name: _____ **Date:** _____

Directions: Study how the words change when you add new endings. Add the same endings to each word to create new words.

1. **sway**   sways   swaying   swayed

   spray _____ _____ _____

   pray   _____ _____ _____

   stray _____ _____ _____

   fray   _____ _____ _____

Directions: Find three words in the Word Bank that are related to each of the spelling words. Write the words on the correct lines.

Word Bank				
grayish	overstay	staying	player	grayer
playful	grayest	playing	stayed	

2. gray _____ _____ _____

3. play _____ _____ _____

4. stay _____ _____ _____

Name: _____ **Date:** _____

Directions: Answer each question in a complete sentence. Turn the question around, and use the bold word in each answer.

1. Why do people **spray** their gardens with pesticides?

   _____

   _____

2. Why should you **stay** in one spot if you lose your parents at the mall?

   _____

   _____

3. What are three things that are **gray**?

   _____

   _____

4. Why do waiters need to use a **tray** to carry food?

   _____

   _____

5. Why do clothes start to **fray**?

   _____

   _____

6. What is your favorite game to **play** at recess and why?

   _____

   _____

Turn the Question Around

Analogies

Name: _____ Date: _____

Directions: Use a word from the Word Bank to complete each analogy.

Word Bank				
away	clay	fray	gray	play
pray	spray	stay	stray	tray

1. **frog** is to **green** as **hippo** is to _____

2. **shovel** is to **dig** as **hose** is to _____

3. **class** is to **learn** as **recess** is to _____

4. **closer** is to **toward** as **farther** is to _____

5. **collage** is to **paper** as **sculpture** is to _____

6. **paper** is to **rip** as **cloth** is to _____

7. **home lunch** is to **lunchbox** as **school lunch** is to _____

8. **push** is to **pull** as **leave** is to _____

9. **mall** is to **shop** as **church** is to _____

10. **dog with tags** is to **pet** as **dog without tags** is to _____

UNIT 15
Long A
Vowel Team *ai*

Focus

This week's focus is one-syllable words that start with a consonant blend and end with *ai* plus a consonant or consonant blend.

Helpful Hint

Notice that the *ai* pattern never appears at the end of a base word or syllable. When spelling, only use the *ai* pattern at the beginning or middle of a word *(aim, brain)*.

- brain
- chair
- frail
- grain
- paint
- plain
- sprain
- trail
- train
- waist

See page 7 for additional spelling activities.

Name: _____ **Date:** _____

Directions: Use a word from the Word Bank to complete each sentence.

Sentence Completions

Word Bank				
brain	chair	frail	grain	paint
plain	sprain	trail	train	waist

1. A bike helmet will protect your _____ if you fall.

2. Please push in your _____ before you line up.

3. We rode our bikes on a dirt _____ .

4. Our _____ left the station at 6:00 p.m.

5. The birthday card looked _____ , so I decided to add more colors and details.

6. If I don't wear a belt around my _____ , these pants will fall down.

7. Bread, rice, and pasta all belong to the _____ group.

8. We had to _____ the walls again after my little brother scribbled on them.

9. My great-grandmother uses a walker because she is old and

_____ .

10. If I try to wear high heels, I will probably _____ my ankle!

Name: _____ **Date:** _____

Directions: Use a word from the Word Bank for each section.

Word Bank				
brain	chair	frail	grain	paint
plain	sprain	trail	train	waist

Write a synonym for each word.

1. twist _____

2. path _____

3. midsection _____

4. add color _____

Write an antonym for each word.

5. fancy _____

6. strong _____

Write a word that fits each category.

7. bus, plane, subway, _____

8. stool, seat, bench, _____

9. protein, dairy, vegetable, _____

10. heart, lungs, kidneys, _____

Name: _____ **Date:** _____

Directions: Sort the words in the Word Bank into two categories: *Singular Nouns* and *Plural Nouns*. Write each word in the correct column.

Word Bank				
brain	chairs	trails	grains	snails
chain	train	waist	braids	paint

Singular Nouns	Plural Nouns
○	○
○	○
○	○
○	○
○	○

Directions: Write all 10 words in ABC order.

1. _____

2. _____

3. _____

4. _____

5. _____

6. _____

7. _____

8. _____

9. _____

10. _____

   28630—180 Days of Spelling and Word Study

Name: _____ **Date:**_____

Directions: Answer each question in a complete sentence. Turn the question around, and use the bold word in each answer.

1. What color would you like to **paint** your bedroom?

_____

_____

2. Why do people wear a belt around their **waist**?

_____

_____

3. Why do you think children should sit in **chairs** while they eat?

_____

_____

4. What are three foods from the **grains** group that you like to eat?

_____

_____

5. What should you do if you **sprain** your ankle?

_____

_____

6. Why do **frail** people sometimes use a walker or cane?

_____

_____

Turn the Question Around

Analogies

Name: _____ **Date:** _____

Directions: Use a word from the Word Bank to complete each analogy.

Word Bank				
brain	chair	frail	grain	paint
plain	sprain	trail	train	waist

1. **lie** is to **bed** as **sit** is to _____

2. **crayon** is to **color** as **brush** is to _____

3. **bracelet** is to **wrist** as **belt** is to _____

4. **chicken** is to **protein** as **rice** is to _____

5. **pilot** is to **plane** as **conductor** is to _____

6. **cast** is to **broken** as **bandage** is to _____

7. **chest** is to **heart** as **head** is to _____

8. **paved** is to **road** as **dirt** is to _____

9. **strong** is to **hardy** as **weak** is to _____

10. **waste** is to **waist** as **plane** is to _____

UNIT 16
Long E Vowel Team ea

➤ cheap

➤ clean

➤ clear

➤ dream

➤ feast

➤ knead

➤ scream

➤ speak

➤ stream

➤ wreath

Focus

This week's focus is one-syllable words that start with a consonant blend or digraph and end with *ea* plus a consonant or digraph.

Helpful Hint

The two most common long *e* patterns are *ea* and *ee*. Unfortunately, there is no trick or rule to help spellers determine which pattern to use since they both appear at the beginning, middle, or end of a word. It's best to try both patterns and see which one "looks" right. The more we read, the easier it is to choose the correct spelling!

See page 7 for additional spelling activities.

Name: _____ **Date:** _____

Directions: Use a word from the Word Bank to complete each sentence.

Word Bank				
cheap	clean	clear	dream	feast
knead	scream	speak	stream	wreath

1. I had a crazy _____ last night.

2. Mom made a _____ out of pinecones and hung it on the front door.

3. Grandma cooked up a huge _____ when my uncle came home from the Army.

4. First, you _____ the dough. Then, you spread it on a pizza stone.

5. It'll take me three hours to _____ my bedroom.

6. Papa's on the phone. Would you like to _____ to him?

7. We spent the day fishing along the _____ .

8. We'll have school tomorrow if it stops snowing and the roads are

   _____ .

9. The headphones were so _____ , they broke the first time I used them.

10. Micah couldn't hear me, so I had to _____ .

Name: _____ **Date:** _____

Directions: Use a word from the Word Bank for each section.

Word Bank				
cheap	clean	clear	dream	feast
knead	scream	speak	stream	wreath

Write a synonym for each word.

1. talk _____

2. see-through _____

3. big meal _____

4. imagine _____

Write an antonym for each word.

5. expensive _____

6. whisper _____

7. dirty _____

Write a word that fits each category.

8. Christmas tree, stockings, mistletoe, _____

9. massage, press, mold, _____

10. river, creek, brook, _____

Inflectional Endings

Name: _____ **Date:** _____

Directions: Study how the words change when you add new endings. Add the same endings to each word to create new words.

1. **lean**   leans   leaning   leaned

   clean _____   _____   _____

2. **scream**   screams   screaming   screamed

   dream _____   _____   _____

3. **bead**   beads   beading   beaded

   knead _____   _____   _____

Directions: Find three words in the Word Bank that are related to each of the spelling words. Write the words on the correct lines.

Word Bank				
cheaper	clearly	spoke	speaking	clearing
cleared	cheapest	cheaply	speaker	

4. cheap _____   _____   _____

5. speak _____   _____   _____

6. clear _____   _____   _____

Name: _____ **Date:** _____

Directions: Change each singular noun to a plural noun. Remember, if a singular noun ends with *ch* or *sh*, add *–es* to make it plural.

Singular Noun	Plural Noun (Add *–es*)
beach	
peach	
leash	
speech	
screech	

Directions: Write the plural of each irregular noun.

Singular Noun	Plural Noun
foot	
tooth	
sheep	
deer	
person	

 Some nouns don't follow the *–s* or *–es* suffix rule. They look and sound like whole new words when they change to the plural. Or, their singular and plural forms look exactly the same. We call these words *irregular nouns*.

Prefixes and Suffixes

Name: _____ Date: _____

Directions: Use a word from the Word Bank to complete each analogy.

Word Bank				
cheap	clean	clear	dream	feast
knead	scream	speak	stream	wreath

1. **stove** is to **cook** as **dishwasher** is to _____

2. **crystal** is to **expensive** as **glass** is to _____

3. **batter** is to **stir** as **dough** is to _____

4. **rock** is to **pebble** as **river** is to _____

5. **awake** is to **imagine** as **asleep** is to _____

6. **Fourth of July** is to **cookout** as **Thanksgiving** is to _____

7. **Christmas tree** is to **ornament** as **door** is to _____

8. **muddy water** is to **murky** as **clean water** is to _____

9. **library** is to **whisper** as **roller coaster** is to _____

10. **hands** is to **sign** as **voice** is to _____

28630—180 Days of Spelling and Word Study

UNIT 17
Long E Vowel Team ee

- ➤ **bleed**
- ➤ **green**
- ➤ **kneel**
- ➤ **screen**
- ➤ **sheet**
- ➤ **sleep**
- ➤ **speech**
- ➤ **street**
- ➤ **teeth**
- ➤ **three**

Focus

This week's focus is one-syllable words that start with a consonant blend or digraph and end with *ee* plus a consonant or digraph.

Helpful Hint

Homophones are words that sound the same but have different spellings and meanings. There are many long *e* homophones in the English language. They sound the same but differ in their use of the *ee* or *ea* pattern (*sea/see, meat/meet*).

See page 7 for additional spelling activities.

Sentence Completions

Name: _____ **Date:** _____

Directions: Use a word from the Word Bank to complete each sentence.

Word Bank				
bleed	green	kneel	screen	sheet
sleep	speech	street	teeth	three

1. I've read _____ books in the series.

2. They've built two new houses on my _____ since June.

3. I helped Mom put a clean _____ on the bed.

4. A spider crawled across the _____ while I was watching TV.

5. Dad says I have a _____ thumb because I'm really good with plants.

6. Remember to brush your _____ at least twice a day.

7. I have to give a _____ in front of the whole school if I run for student council.

8. Don't pick at your scabs or they will start to _____ .

9. I can't go to _____ without my nightlight.

10. I had to _____ in the front row when we took our class photo.

Name: _____ **Date:** _____

Directions: Use a word from the Word Bank for each section.

Word Bank

bleed	green	kneel	screen	sheet
sleep	speech	street	teeth	three

Write a synonym for each word.

1. molars _____

2. road _____

3. blanket _____

4. mesh cover _____

Write an antonym for each word.

5. wake up _____

6. heal _____

Write a word that fits each category.

7. blue, black, orange, _____

8. five, eight, nine, _____

9. stand, sit, squat, _____

10. presentation, talk, lecture, _____

Homophones

Name: _____ **Date:** _____

Directions: Homophones sound the same but have different spellings and meanings. Write the correct homophone on each line.

1. My sister can't _____ the board without her glasses.
    (sea/see)

2. I can't believe you _____ me again at checkers!
    (beat/beet)

3. Kyle missed a whole _____ of school when he
    was sick.
    (weak/week)

4. I _____ to get something out of my backpack.
    (knead/need)

5. Put this ointment on your cuts to help them _____ .
    (heal/heel)

6. Would you like to _____ a movie star?
    (meat/meet)

7. We saw three _____ eating grass near the road.
    (dear/deer)

8. Did your coach tell you to _____ home?
    (steal/steel)

9. Mom had to rip out the _____ of my costume and
    sew them again.
    (seams/seems)

10. Ouch! I think I just got stung by a _____ !
    (be/bee)

Name: _____ **Date:** _____

Directions: Answer each question in a complete sentence. Turn the question around, and use the bold word in each answer.

1. What should you do if your knee starts to **bleed**?

   _____

   _____

2. Why is it important to look both ways before you cross the **street**?

   _____

   _____

3. Why do children lose their baby **teeth**?

   _____

   _____

4. What three things are **green**?

   _____

   _____

5. Why is it important to get a good night's **sleep**?

   _____

   _____

6. Why do you think parents should limit their kids' **screen** time?

   _____

   _____

Analogies

Name: _____ **Date:** _____

Directions: Use a word from the Word Bank to complete each analogy.

Word Bank				
bleed	green	kneel	screen	sheet
sleep	speech	street	teeth	three

1. **lick** is to **tongue** as **bite** is to _____

2. **sun** is to **yellow** as **grass** is to _____

3. **feet** is to **stand** as **knees** is to _____

4. **square** is to **four** as **triangle** is to _____

5. **window** is to **curtain** as **bed** is to _____

6. **kitchen** is to **eat** as **bedroom** is to _____

7. **bike** is to **path** as **car** is to _____

8. **glass** is to **window** as **mesh** is to _____

9. **singer** is to **song** as **speaker** is to _____

10. **stomach** is to **ache** as **nose** is to _____

UNIT 18
Long *I* Patterns
igh, ild, ind

WEEK 18

- blind
- bright
- child
- find
- flight
- fright
- grind
- knight
- mighty
- slight

Focus

This week's focus is long *i* patterns in one-syllable words. The *igh, ild,* and *ind* patterns are introduced.

Helpful Hint

A vowel is usually short when it appears by itself in the middle of a one-syllable word *(fast, mint)*. This is not true for most *ild* and *ind* words, though. In these words, the *i* sound is usually long *(find, mild)*.

See page 7 for additional spelling activities.

Sentence Completions

Name: _____ **Date:** _____

Directions: Use a word from the Word Bank to complete each sentence.

Word Bank				
blind	bright	child	find	flight
fright	grind	knight	mighty	slight

1. There was only a _____ breeze at the beach today.

2. My dad likes to _____ his coffee beans in the morning.

3. We have a new _____ in our class.

4. Our _____ was delayed because of bad weather.

5. Can you help me _____ my missing glove?

6. My neighbor needs a service dog to help her because she's

   _____ .

7. The king sent his bravest _____ to slay the dragon.

8. It would take a _____ wind to knock over this old oak tree.

9. I turned pale with _____ when I saw my friend fall from the top of the slide.

10. Please turn off that _____ light. I'm trying to sleep!

Name: _____ Date:_____

Directions: Use a word from the Word Bank for each section.

Word Bank				
blind	bright	child	find	flight
fright	grind	knight	mighty	slight

Write a synonym for each word.

1. soldier _____

2. crush _____

3. powerful _____

4. fear _____

Write an antonym for each word.

5. able to see _____

6. major _____

7. lose _____

8. dim _____

Write a word that fits each category.

9. voyage, journey, trip, _____

10. kid, tot, youth, _____

Name: _____ **Date:** _____

Directions: Adding the suffix –er or –est to an adjective changes its meaning. The –er suffix means *more*, and –est means *most*. Add two suffixes to each adjective.

Adjective	Add –er	Add –est
high		
light		
tight		
bright		
mild		
kind		

Directions: Use a word from the chart to fill in each blank.

1. These pants are _____ than the ones I wore yesterday. I can't even button them.

2. Emma is the _____ person I know. She is nice to everyone.

3. This flashlight shines _____ than the other one.

4. I asked the waiter if he had a _____ salsa because the first one was too spicy.

5. I climbed up to the _____ rung of the ladder.

Name: _____ Date: _____

Directions: Sort the words in the Word Bank into two categories: *Adjectives* and *Nouns.* Write each word in the correct column.

Word Bank				
slight	nightlight	bright	child	thigh
mighty	blind	knight	kind	flight

Adjectives	Nouns
○	○
○	○
○	○
○	○
○	○

Directions: Write all 10 words in ABC order.

1. _____   6. _____

2. _____   7. _____

3. _____   8. _____

4. _____   9. _____

5. _____   10. _____

Word Sorts

Analogies

Name: _____ **Date:** _____

Directions: Use a word from the Word Bank to complete each analogy.

Word Bank				
blind	bright	child	find	flight
fright	grind	knight	mighty	slight

1. **cheese** is to **grate** as **pepper** is to _____

2. **uniform** is to **soldier** as **armor** is to _____

3. **joke book** is to **laughter** as **ghost story** is to _____

4. **ship** is to **voyage** as **airplane** is to _____

5. **candlelight** is to **dim** as **spotlight** is to _____

6. **people** is to **person** as **children** is to _____

7. **breeze** is to **gentle** as **hurricane wind** is to _____

8. **lion** is to **large** as **bird** is to _____

9. **ears** is to **deaf** as **eyes** is to _____

10. **hide** is to **seek** as **lose** is to _____

UNIT 19
Long O Vowel Team oa

Focus

This week's focus is one-syllable words that start with a consonant blend and end with *oa* plus a consonant or consonant blend.

Helpful Hint

Notice that the *oa* pattern is only used at the beginning or middle of a base word, never at the end. When you need to write the long *o* sound at the end of a word, use *ow* instead.

➤ **boast**
➤ **coach**
➤ **coast**
➤ **croak**
➤ **float**
➤ **groan**
➤ **oath**
➤ **roast**
➤ **throat**
➤ **toast**

See page 7 for additional spelling activities.

Sentence Completions

Name: _____ **Date:** _____

Directions: Use a word from the Word Bank to complete each sentence.

Word Bank				
boast	coach	coast	croak	float
groan	oath	roast	throat	toast

1. The turkey needs to _____ in the oven for at least two more hours.

2. Dad threw me a pool noodle so I could _____ .

3. Why do you _____ and flop on the floor when it's time to clean your room?

4. No one wants to hear you _____ about all your soccer trophies.

5. Mom took me to the doctor because I had a fever and sore

   _____ .

6. When you take an _____ , you promise to tell the truth on the witness stand.

7. My _____ showed me how to swing a bat.

8. On warm summer nights, we can hear frogs _____ in our pond.

9. The best man held up his glass and made a _____ to the bride and groom.

10. We traveled up the Pacific _____ .

Name: _____ **Date:** _____

Directions: Use a word from the Word Bank for each section.

Word Bank				
boast	coach	coast	croak	float
groan	oath	roast	throat	toast

Write a synonym for each word.

1. brag _____

2. promise _____

3. shoreline _____

Write an antonym for each word.

4. sink _____

5. player _____

6. cheer _____

Write a word that fits each category.

7. chirp, squawk, tweet, _____

8. eggs, bacon, hash browns, _____

9. mouth, stomach, intestines, _____

10. grill, bake, fry, _____

Name: _____ **Date:** _____

Directions: Study how the words change when you add new endings. Add the same endings to each word to create new words.

1. poach   poaches   poaching   poached

   coach _____   _____   _____

2. loan   loans   loaning   loaned

   groan _____   _____   _____

3. roast   roasts   roasting   roasted

   boast _____   _____   _____

Directions: Find three words in the Word Bank that are related to each of the spelling words. Write the words on the correct lines.

Word Bank				
toaster	roasted	afloat	toasted	roaster
floating	roasting	toasty	floaty	

4. float _____   _____   _____

5. roast _____   _____   _____

6. toast _____   _____   _____

Name: _____ **Date:** _____

Directions: Answer each question in a complete sentence. Turn the question around, and use the bold word in each answer.

1. Why do people like to visit the **coast**?

   _____

   _____

2. Why do kids **groan** when they eat too many sweets?

   _____

   _____

3. Why is it important to listen to your **coach**?

   _____

   _____

4. What makes a sore **throat** feel better?

   _____

   _____

5. What is your favorite kind of **toast**?

   _____

   _____

6. What can people use to help them **float** in a pool?

   _____

   _____

Turn the Question Around

Analogies

Name: _____ Date: _____

Directions: Use a word from the Word Bank to complete each analogy.

Word Bank				
boast	coach	coast	croak	float
groan	oath	roast	throat	toast

1. **cricket** is to **chirp** as **frog** is to _____

2. **class** is to **teacher** as **team** is to _____

3. **stuffy** is to **nose** as **sore** is to _____

4. **cream cheese** is to **bagel** as **butter** is to _____

5. **sadness** is to **whimper** as **pain** is to _____

6. **uphill** is to **pedal** as **downhill** is to _____

7. **classroom** is to **pledge** as **courtroom** is to _____

8. **anchor** is to **sink** as **buoy** is to _____

9. **toaster** is to **toast** as **oven** is to _____

10. **"You're awesome"** is to **compliment** as **"I'm awesome"** is to

_____

UNIT 20
Long O Vowel Team ow

Focus

This week's focus is one-syllable long *o* words that start with a consonant blend and end with *–ow*.

Helpful Hint

Notice that the *ow* pattern usually appears at the end of a word. When you need to write the long *o* sound in the middle of a syllable, use *oa* instead. (*Own* is an exception.)

- ➤ **blow**
- ➤ **flow**
- ➤ **glow**
- ➤ **grow**
- ➤ **know**
- ➤ **own**
- ➤ **slow**
- ➤ **snow**
- ➤ **stow**
- ➤ **throw**

See page 7 for additional spelling activities.

Sentence Completions

Name: _____ Date:_____

Directions: Use a word from the Word Bank to complete each sentence.

Word Bank				
blow	flow	glow	grow	know
own	slow	snow	stow	throw

1. Please _____ your dirty clothes in the hamper.

2. Does the writing on your T-shirt _____ in the dark?

3. We're renting an apartment right now, but someday we'll

   _____ a house.

4. Do you _____ how to get to the mall from here?

5. Yesterday, we went sledding in the _____ .

6. Make a wish before you _____ out the candles!

7. Does this river _____ all the way to the ocean?

8. Sunlight, water, and rich soil help plants _____ .

9. You can _____ your bag under the seat or in the overhead compartment.

10. You need to _____ down when you drive through a neighborhood.

Name: _____ **Date:** _____

Directions: Use a word from the Word Bank for each section.

Word Bank				
blow	flow	glow	grow	know
own	slow	snow	stow	throw

Write a synonym for each word.

1. toss _____

2. stash _____

3. light up _____

4. possess _____

Write an antonym for each word.

5. shrink _____

6. fast _____

Write a word that fits each category.

7. rain, sleet, hail, _____

8. whistle, exhale, puff, _____

9. think, believe, realize, _____

10. spill out, pour, ooze, _____

Inflectional Endings

Name: _____ **Date:** _____

Directions: Study how the words change when you add new endings. Add the same endings to each word to create new words.

1. **blow**   blows   blowing   blew

   grow   _____   _____   _____

   know   _____   _____   _____

   throw _____   _____   _____

2. **snow**   snows   snowing   snowed

   show   _____   _____   _____

   flow   _____   _____   _____

Directions: Find three words in the Word Bank that are related to each of the spelling words. Write the words on the correct lines.

Word Bank				
knowledge	owner	snowball	snowflake	owned
owns	known	snowfall	unknown	

3. own   _____   _____   _____

4. know _____   _____   _____

5. snow _____   _____   _____

Name: _____ **Date:**_____

Directions: Sort the words in the Word Bank into two categories: *Present Tense Verbs* and *Past Tense Verbs.* Write each word in the correct column.

Word Bank				
blew	snowed	own	flow	grew
knew	glow	showed	throw	stow

Present Tense Verbs	Past Tense Verbs
○	○
○	○
○	○
○	○
○	○

Directions: Write all 10 words in ABC order.

1. _____
2. _____
3. _____
4. _____
5. _____

6. _____
7. _____
8. _____
9. _____
10. _____

Analogies

Name: _____ **Date:** _____

Directions: Use a word from the Word Bank to complete each analogy.

Word Bank				
blow	flow	glow	grow	know
own	slow	snow	stow	throw

1. **spring** is to **rain** as **winter** is to _____

2. **cheetah** is to **fast** as **snail** is to _____

3. **soccer ball** is to **kick** as **football** is to _____

4. **birthday cake** is to **eat** as **birthday candle** is to _____

5. **icicles** is to **drip** as **rivers** is to _____

6. **cricket** is to **chirp** as **firefly** is to _____

7. **check out books** is to **borrow** as **buy books** is to _____

8. **on the desk** is to **display** as **in the desk** is to _____

9. **opinion** is to **think** as **fact** is to _____

10. **get smaller** is to **shrink** as **get bigger** is to _____

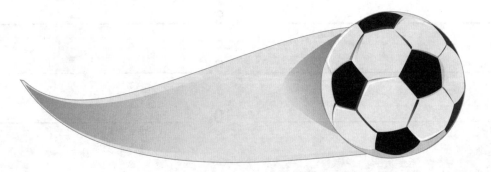

UNIT 21
Long O Patterns
old, olt, ost

Focus

This week's focus is long *o* patterns in one-syllable words.

Helpful Hint

A vowel is usually short when it appears by itself in the middle of a one-syllable word *(pond, fist)*. This is not true for *old* and *olt* words, though. In these words, the *o* sound is long *(scold, volt)*. As you'll notice in a later unit, the *ost* pattern has two sounds *(post, cost)*.

➤ **bolt**

➤ **both**

➤ **cold**

➤ **fold**

➤ **hold**

➤ **mold**

➤ **most**

➤ **post**

➤ **sold**

➤ **told**

See page 7 for additional spelling activities.

Name: _____ **Date:** _____

Directions: Use a word from the Word Bank to complete each sentence.

Word Bank				
bolt	both	cold	fold	hold
mold	most	post	sold	told

Sentence Completions

1. Kids should not _____ their names, ages, or addresses online.

2. I helped my sister _____ and put away all the clean towels.

3. We lost a _____ when we were assembling my new desk.

4. Can you _____ my purse while I try on clothes?

5. I got mud on _____ of my sneakers when I walked on the path.

6. Mom _____ my old bedroom set online.

7. The bread started to _____ , so I threw it out.

8. Wear a hat and mittens so you don't get _____ at the bus stop.

9. Dad _____ us a story about the day he met Mom.

10. I finished _____ of my homework before I left for Cub Scouts.

Name: _____ **Date:** _____

Directions: Use a word from the Word Bank for each section.

Word Bank				
bolt	both	cold	fold	hold
mold	most	post	sold	told

Write a synonym for each word.

1. almost all _____

2. bend _____

3. informed _____

4. grasp _____

Write an antonym for each word.

5. neither _____

6. hot _____

7. bought _____

Write a word that fits each category.

8. screw, nut, washer, _____

9. moss, fungus, scum, _____

10. pole, stake, pillar, _____

 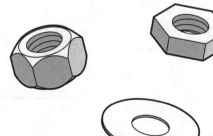  

Name: _____ **Date:** _____

Directions: Study how the words change when you add new endings. Add the same endings to each word to create new words.

1. **sell**   sells   selling   sold

   tell   _____   _____   _____

2. **host**   hosts   hosting   hosted

   post   _____   _____   _____

3. **mold**   molds   molding   molded

   fold   _____   _____   _____

Directions: Find three words in the Word Bank that are related to each of the words. Write the words on the correct lines.

Word Bank				
held	combs	colder	combing	holding
holder	coldest	coldness	honeycomb	

4. hold   _____   _____   _____

5. cold   _____   _____   _____

6. comb   _____   _____   _____

28630—180 Days of Spelling and Word Study   © *Shell Education*

Name: _____ **Date:** _____

Directions: Adverbs describe a verb. They tell how an action is done. Adding –ly to some adjectives turns them into adverbs. Add –ly to each adjective.

Adjective	Adverb (Add –ly)
cold	
bold	
slow	
kind	
light	
shy	

Directions: Use a word from the chart to fill in each blank.

1. Our school nurse always acts _____ toward kids and makes them feel welcome.

2. Erase your mistakes _____ so you don't rip the paper.

3. The little girl hid _____ behind her mom on the first day of preschool.

4. Abe stepped forward and _____ declared, "I'll catch the mouse!"

5. We walked _____ back to the line because we didn't want recess to end.

Analogies

Name: _____ **Date:** _____

Directions: Use a word from the Word Bank to complete each analogy.

Word Bank				
bolt	both	cold	fold	hold
mold	most	post	sold	told

1. **fire** is to **hot** as **ice** is to _____

2. **apple** is to **rot** as **cheese** is to _____

3. **clean dishes** is to **stack** as **clean laundry** is to _____

4. **power lines** is to **pole** as **mailbox** is to _____

5. **apartment** is to **rented** as **house** is to _____

6. **sell** is to **sold** as **tell** is to _____

7. **less** is to **least** as **more** is to _____

8. **hammer** is to **nail** as **wrench** is to _____

9. **zero** is to **neither** as **two** is to _____

10. **spout** is to **pour** as **handle** is to _____

UNIT 22
Long U Pattern oo

Focus

This week's focus is one-syllable long *u* words that start with a consonant blend and end with *oo* plus a consonant or consonant digraph.

Helpful Hint

Notice that *ch* makes a /k/ sound in words such as *school* and *schooner*.

- ➤ **bloom**
- ➤ **booth**
- ➤ **broom**
- ➤ **droop**
- ➤ **groom**
- ➤ **school**
- ➤ **scoop**
- ➤ **smooth**
- ➤ **spoon**
- ➤ **tooth**

See page 7 for additional spelling activities.

Name: _____ **Date:** _____

Directions: Use a word from the Word Bank to complete each sentence.

Word Bank				
bloom	booth	broom	droop	groom
school	scoop	smooth	spoon	tooth

1. I lost my first _____ when I was in kindergarten.

2. You need to eat your soup with a _____ .

3. I noticed that the tulips always _____ on my mom's birthday.

4. Nevaeh missed the bus, so her dad drove her to

   _____ .

5. If you forget to water the flowers, their leaves will start to

   _____ .

6. Use a _____ to sweep up all these crumbs.

7. Would you like one _____ of ice cream or two?

8. The _____ stood in front of the altar and waited for his bride.

9. You can pick up your tickets at the _____ in the front of the theater.

10. I brushed my dog's fur until it was _____ and shiny.

Sentence Completions

Name: _____ **Date:** _____

Directions: Use a word from the Word Bank for each section.

Word Bank				
bloom	booth	broom	droop	groom
school	scoop	smooth	spoon	tooth

Write a synonym for each word.

1. sag _____

2. blossom _____

3. small room _____

4. dig into _____

Write an antonym for each word.

5. bumpy _____

6. bride _____

Write a word that fits each category.

7. knife, fork, spatula, _____

8. tongue, lips, gums, _____

9. mop, vacuum, duster, _____

10. town hall, police station, fire station, _____

Name: _____ **Date:** _____

Directions: Study how the words change when you add new endings. Add the same endings to each word to create new words.

1. **loop**   loops   looping   looped

   scoop _____   _____   _____

   droop _____   _____   _____

2. **zoom**   zooms   zooming   zoomed

   bloom _____   _____   _____

   groom _____   _____   _____

Directions: Find three words in the Word Bank that are related to each of the spelling words. Write the words on the correct lines.

Word Bank				
toothbrush	preschool	teaspoon	tablespoon	toothpaste
schoolhouse	spoonful	teeth	schoolwork	

3. spoon _____   _____   _____

4. tooth _____   _____   _____

5. school _____   _____   _____

Name: _____ **Date:** _____

Directions: Answer each question in a complete sentence. Turn the question around, and use the bold word in each answer.

1. Why do people stand in a **booth** when they vote?

   _____

   _____

2. What do you do when you lose a **tooth**?

   _____

   _____

3. Why do people keep a **broom** near the kitchen?

   _____

   _____

4. What is your favorite subject at **school** and why?

   _____

   _____

5. Why do plants start to **droop**?

   _____

   _____

6. How does lotion help keep hands **smooth**?

   _____

   _____

Name: _____ **Date:** _____

Directions: Use a word from the Word Bank to complete each analogy.

Word Bank				
bloom	booth	broom	droop	groom
school	scoop	smooth	spoon	tooth

1. **heal** is to **hospital** as **learn** is to _____

2. **cake** is to **slice** as **ice cream** is to _____

3. **cake** is to **fork** as **ice cream** is to _____

4. **lick** is to **tongue** as **bite** is to _____

5. **wife** is to **bride** as **husband** is to _____

6. **food** is to **snack bar** as **tickets** is to _____

7. **scrub** is to **sponge** as **sweep** is to _____

8. **well-rested** is to **stand tall** as **tired** is to _____

9. **fleece** is to **fuzzy** as **silk** is to _____

10. **fruit** is to **ripen** as **flower** is to _____

UNIT 23

Long U Patterns
eu, ew, and ui

Focus

This week's focus is one-syllable long *u* words that start with a consonant blend and end with *–ew* or *–ue*. The *ui* pattern is introduced.

Helpful Hint

The vowel teams *ew* and *ue* almost always appear at the end of a word or syllable (*jew·el, glue*). Therefore, spellers need to rely on their visual memory to determine which pattern to use in a particular word.

- ➤ blew
- ➤ crew
- ➤ drew
- ➤ fruit
- ➤ grew
- ➤ knew
- ➤ screw
- ➤ suit
- ➤ threw
- ➤ true

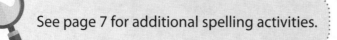

See page 7 for additional spelling activities.

Sentence Completions

Name: _____ **Date:** _____

Directions: Use a word from the Word Bank to complete each sentence.

Word Bank				
blew	crew	drew	fruit	grew
knew	screw	suit	threw	true

1. My flowers _____ much faster after I watered them.

2. I _____ it would rain on my birthday!

3. Please hand me the _____ so I can finish putting this desk together.

4. The pitcher _____ 10 strikes in a row.

5. The captain and his _____ set sail on Monday.

6. Is it _____ that snakes don't have eyelids?

7. Steph _____ a picture of her family with crayons.

8. Would you like a piece of _____ in your lunchbox?

9. Adeline _____ out the candles and made a wish.

10. Bring your bathing _____ to the pool party.

28630—180 Days of Spelling and Word Study

Name: _____ **Date:** _____

Directions: Use a word from the Word Bank for each section.

Word Bank				
blew	crew	drew	fruit	grew
knew	screw	suit	threw	true

Write a synonym for each word.

1. group of workers _____

2. sketched _____

3. clothing set _____

Write an antonym for each word.

4. false _____

5. caught _____

6. shrank _____

7. forgot _____

Write a word that fits each category.

8. vegetable, dairy, grain, _____

9. nail, bolt, pin, _____

10. gusted, howled, blustered, _____

Word Sorts

Name: _____ **Date:** _____

Directions: Sort the words in the Word Bank into two categories: *Present Tense Verbs* and *Past Tense Verbs.* Write each word in the correct column.

Word Bank				
glued	blow	know	drew	bloom
flew	grow	threw	droop	chewed

Present Tense Verbs	Past Tense Verbs
○	○
○	○
○	○
○	○
○	○

Directions: Write all 10 words in ABC order.

1. _____   6. _____

2. _____   7. _____

3. _____   8. _____

4. _____   9. _____

5. _____   10. _____

Name: _____ **Date:**_____

Directions: Answer each question in a complete sentence. Turn the question around, and use the bold word in each answer.

1. Why should we keep **screws** away from babies and toddlers?

   _____

   _____

2. Why do most teachers like **glue** sticks better than glue bottles?

   _____

   _____

3. What types of **clues** do police look for at a crime scene?

   _____

   _____

4. Which **fruit** is your favorite? Why?

   _____

   _____

5. What is the last picture you **drew**?

   _____

   _____

6. What is a **true** statement about your family?

   _____

   _____

Analogies

Name: _____ **Date:** _____

Directions: Use a word from the Word Bank to complete each analogy.

Word Bank				
blew	crew	drew	fruit	grew
knew	screw	suit	threw	true

1. **hammer** is to **nail** as **screwdriver** is to _____

2. **carrot** is to **vegetable** as **apple** is to _____

3. **lady** is to **gown** as **man** is to _____

4. **sun** is to **shone** as **wind** is to _____

5. **onstage** is to **actors** as **backstage** is to _____

6. **shrink** is to **shrank** as **grow** is to _____

7. **baseball** is to **tossed** as **basketball** is to _____

8. **brush** is to **painted** as **pencil** is to _____

9. **blue** is to **blew** as **new** is to _____

10. **dogs are reptiles** is to **false** as **dogs are mammals** is to

_____

UNIT 24
ou Diphthong

Focus

This week's focus is one-syllable words that contain *ou* and an initial or final blend.

Helpful Hint

The diphthong *ou (ouch, proud)* can be found at the beginning or middle of many words, but never at the end.

➤ **around**

➤ **cloud**

➤ **count**

➤ **crouch**

➤ **flour**

➤ **found**

➤ **ground**

➤ **proud**

➤ **sound**

➤ **sprout**

See page 7 for additional spelling activities.

Name: _____ **Date:**_____

Directions: Use a word from the Word Bank to complete each sentence.

Word Bank				
around	cloud	count	crouch	flour
found	ground	proud	sound	sprout

1. I was _____ of myself for going on the scary roller coaster.

2. How much _____ do you need for the recipe?

3. The first buds started poking through the _____ in March.

4. We drove _____ the lot three times looking for a parking space.

5. Dad had to _____ down to fit through our tree house door.

6. I _____ a set of keys lying in the grass.

7. Can you help me _____ up the money we earned at the bake sale?

8. It was a beautiful day. There wasn't a single _____ in the sky.

9. All of our bean plants started to _____ at the same time.

10. I love the _____ of a baby laughing.

Name: _____ **Date:** _____

Directions: Use a word from the Word Bank for each section.

Word Bank				
around	cloud	count	crouch	flour
found	ground	proud	sound	sprout

Write a synonym for each word.

1. noise _____

2. bud _____

3. squat _____

4. add up _____

Write an antonym for each word.

5. lost _____

6. ashamed _____

7. sky _____

Write a word that fits each category.

8. over, under, through, _____

9. sugar, salt, baking soda, _____

10. mist, fog, steam, _____

SUGAR

FLOUR

Name: _____ **Date:** _____

Directions: Study how the words change when you add new endings. Add the same endings to each word to create new words.

1. **bind**   binds   binding   bound

   grind _____ _____ _____

   find _____ _____ _____

2. **mount**   mounts   mounting   mounted

   count _____ _____ _____

3. **pout**   pouts   pouting   pouted

   sprout _____ _____ _____

Directions: Find three words in the Word Bank that are related to each of the spelling words. Write the words on the correct lines.

Word Bank				
cloudy	crouches	crouching	proudly	prouder
clouds	proudest	cloudless	crouched	

4. **proud** _____ _____ _____

5. **cloud** _____ _____ _____

6. **crouch** _____ _____ _____

Name: _____ **Date:** _____

Directions: Adverbs describe a verb. They tell how an action is done. Adding –ly to some adjectives turns them into adverbs. Add –ly to each adjective.

Adjective	Adverb (Add –ly)
loud	
proud	
rude	
smooth	
glad	
sad	

Directions: Use a word from the chart to complete each blank.

1. A boy _____ pushed in front of me in line yesterday.

2. Nico _____ buried his goldfish in the backyard.

3. I will _____ trade you three grapes for a strawberry.

4. The vendor yelled _____ , "Get your ice cold sodas here!"

5. I hung my report card _____ on the refrigerator.

6. Traffic was moving _____ until we hit New York City.

Analogies

Name: _____ Date: _____

Directions: Use a word from the Word Bank to complete each analogy.

Word Bank				
around	cloud	count	crouch	flour
found	ground	proud	sound	sprout

1. **came** is to **went** as **lost** is to _____

2. **baby** is to **is born** as **seed** is to _____

3. **c-a-t** is to **spell** as **1-2-3** is to _____

4. **low** is to **fog** as **high** is to _____

5. **wet ingredient** is to **milk** as **dry ingredient** is to _____

6. **suspenders** is to **over** as **belt** is to _____

7. **eels** is to **water** as **worms** is to _____

8. **bad grades** is to **disappointed** as **good grades** is to

_____

9. **eyes** is to **sight** as **ears** is to _____

10. **high** is to **on tiptoe** as **low** is to _____

UNIT 25
ow Diphthong

Focus

This week's focus is one- and two-syllable words that contain *ow* and an initial or final blend.

Helpful Hint

A common spelling for the */ow/* diphthong is *ow*. The *ow* pattern appears frequently at the end of a word or syllable *(flow·er, plow)*. It only appears in the middle of a syllable when it precedes *n (brown)*, *d (crowd)*, or *l (howl)*.

- clown
- crowd
- crown
- drown
- flower
- growl
- plow
- powder
- prowl
- scowl

See page 7 for additional spelling activities.

Sentence Completions

Name: _____ Date: _____

Directions: Use a word from the Word Bank to complete each sentence.

Word Bank				
clown	crowd	crown	drown	flower
growl	plow	powder	prowl	scowl

1. Did you like the _____ with the wig and red nose?

2. Sam took lipstick and _____ out of her purse.

3. Which _____ in the garden is your favorite?

4. Don't _____ at me. You're the one who made the big mess!

5. The queen's _____ had diamonds and rubies.

6. If you take away the dog's toy, he'll _____ at you.

7. There was a large _____ of people waiting to get into the theater.

8. Be careful not to _____ your plant with too much water.

9. Sometimes, raccoons _____ near our garbage cans, looking for food.

10. I hope the _____ comes and clears our road soon so we can get out.

Name: _____ **Date:** _____

Directions: Use a word from the Word Bank for each section.

Word Bank				
clown	crowd	crown	drown	flower
growl	plow	powder	prowl	scowl

Write a synonym for each word.

1. group of people _____

2. sneak around _____

3. dirty look _____

4. tiara _____

Write an antonym for this word.

5. swim _____

Write a word that fits each category.

6. bark, snarl, grumble, _____

7. lion tamer, acrobat, tightrope walker, _____

8. lipstick, eyeliner, blush, _____

9. tractor, backhoe, planter, _____

10. bloom, blossom, bud, _____

Synonyms and Antonyms

Inflectional Endings

Name: _____ **Date:** _____

Directions: Study how the words change when you add new endings. Add the same endings to each word to create new words.

1. **frown**   frowns   frowning   frowned

   drown _____   _____   _____

2. **howl**   howls   howling   howled

   scowl _____   _____   _____

   growl _____   _____   _____

   prowl _____   _____   _____

Directions: Find three words in the Word Bank that are related to each of the spelling words. Write the words on the correct lines.

Word Bank				
crowded	powdery	powdered	overcrowding	flowery
sunflower	powders	flowerpot	crowds	

3. powder _____   _____   _____

4. flower _____   _____   _____

5. crowd _____   _____   _____

Name: _____ **Date:**_____

Directions: Answer each question in a complete sentence. Turn the question around, and use the bold word in each answer.

1. What are three reasons someone might send **flowers** to a friend?

   _____

   _____

2. Why do **plows** have sharp edges?

   _____

   _____

3. What should you do if a dog **growls** at you?

   _____

   _____

4. What can kids do to protect themselves from **drowning**?

   _____

   _____

5. Why do some ladies put **powder** on their faces?

   _____

   _____

6. Why are so many people afraid of **clowns**?

   _____

   _____

Analogies

Name: _____ **Date:** _____

Directions: Use a word from the Word Bank to complete each analogy.

Word Bank				
clown	crowd	crown	drown	flower
growl	plow	powder	prowl	scowl

1. **eyelashes** is to **mascara** as **face** is to _____

2. **leaf** is to **stem** as **petal** is to _____

3. **bride** is to **veil** as **queen** is to _____

4. **concert** is to **singer** as **circus** is to _____

5. **sidewalk** is to **shovel** as **road** is to _____

6. **firefighter** is to **burn** as **lifeguard** is to _____

7. **cat** is to **hiss** as **dog** is to _____

8. **joy** is to **grin** as **anger** is to _____

9: **security guard** is to **patrol** as **burglar** is to _____

10. **many cars** is to **traffic** as **many people** is to _____

28630—180 Days of Spelling and Word Study

UNIT 26
oi/oy Diphthongs

Focus

This week's focus is one- and two-syllable words that contain *oi* in the middle of a syllable or *oy* at the end of a syllable.

Helpful Hint

There are two common spellings for the diphthong /oy/: *oi* and *oy*. Notice that *oi* always appears at the beginning *(oil)* or middle of a syllable *(join)*. The *oy* pattern always appears at the end of a word *(joy)* or syllable *(foy·er)*.

- ➤ **broil**
- ➤ **cowboy**
- ➤ **hoist**
- ➤ **joint**
- ➤ **moist**
- ➤ **ploy**
- ➤ **point**
- ➤ **spoil**
- ➤ **tinfoil**
- ➤ **topsoil**

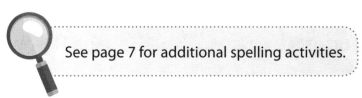

See page 7 for additional spelling activities.

Name: _____ **Date:**_____

Directions: Use a word from the Word Bank to complete each sentence.

Word Bank				
broil	cowboy	hoist	joint	moist
ploy	point	spoil	tinfoil	topsoil

1. Be careful with that pencil. It has a sharp _____ .

2. Nana has a lot of _____ pain in her knee.

3. If you leave meat on the counter all day, it will _____ .

4. Dad likes to _____ the steak until it gets dark and crispy.

5. Uncle Joseph taught me how to _____ the sails on his boat.

6. We need to spread some _____ before we can plant grass here.

7. His hugs and kisses were part of a _____ to stay up past his bedtime.

8. Please wrap the leftover food in _____ and put it in the fridge.

9. If you bake the brownies too long, they won't be

   _____ .

10. My brother dressed up as a _____ on Halloween.

Name: _____ **Date:** _____

Directions: Use a word from the Word Bank for each section.

Word Bank				
broil	cowboy	hoist	joint	moist
ploy	point	spoil	tinfoil	topsoil

Write a synonym for each word.

1. lift up _____

2. wrangler _____

3. dirt _____

4. meeting place _____

Write an antonym for each word.

5. stay fresh _____

6. blunt tip _____

7. dry _____

Write a word that fits each category.

8. trick, scheme, strategy, _____

9. plastic wrap, baggy, wax paper, _____

10. bake, roast, grill, _____

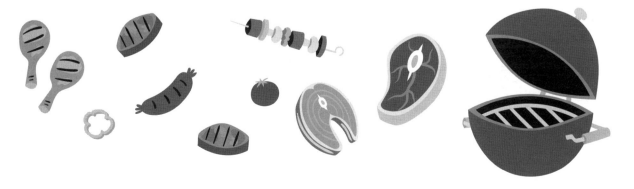

Word Sorts

Name: _____ **Date:** _____

Directions: Sort the words in the Word Bank into two categories: *Compound Words* and *Not Compound Words*. Write each word in the correct column.

Word Bank

tinfoil	point	spoiled	cowboy	ploys
topsoil	voicemail	soybean	moisten	broiling

Compound Words	Not Compound Words
○	○
○	○
○	○
○	○
○	○

Directions: Write all 10 words in ABC order.

1. _____   6. _____

2. _____   7. _____

3. _____   8. _____

4. _____   9. _____

5. _____   10. _____

Name: _____ **Date:**_____

Directions: Answer each question in a complete sentence. Turn the question around, and use the bold word in each answer.

1. How do you **hoist** a flag up the flagpole?

   _____

   _____

2. How can you tell if meat is **spoiled**?

   _____

   _____

3. Why do **cowboys** need a wide brim hat?

   _____

   _____

4. How can people keep their skin **moist**?

   _____

   _____

5. Why is **topsoil** good for plants?

   _____

   _____

6. Why is it rude to **point** at others?

   _____

   _____

Turn the Question Around

Analogies

Name: _____ **Date:**_____

Directions: Use a word from the Word Bank to complete each analogy.

Word Bank				
broil	cowboy	hoist	joint	moist
ploy	point	spoil	tinfoil	topsoil

1. **bread** is to **mold** as **meat** is to _____

2. **yogurt** is to **creamy** as **brownie** is to _____

3. **sheet** is to **blanket** as **plastic wrap** is to _____

4. **oars** is to **row** as **sails** is to _____

5. **sheep** is to **shepherd** as **cattle** is to _____

6. **spaghetti** is to **boil** as **steak** is to _____

7. **crabs** is to **sand** as **bugs** is to _____

8. **plan** is to **strategy** as **scheme** is to _____

9. **hand** is to **wave** as **finger** is to _____

10. **heart** is to **organ** as **knee** is to _____

UNIT 27

/Ô/ Pattern with O

Focus

This week's focus is one-syllable words that use *o* to make the */aw/* sound and contain an initial or final blend.

Helpful Hint

Notice that the *o* in these words does not make a short *o* sound. Instead, it has a lower, back-of-the-mouth sound that rhymes with */aw/*.

- ➤ **broth**
- ➤ **cloth**
- ➤ **cost**
- ➤ **cross**
- ➤ **floss**
- ➤ **frost**
- ➤ **froth**
- ➤ **gloss**
- ➤ **lost**
- ➤ **soft**

See page 7 for additional spelling activities.

Name: _____ **Date:** _____

Directions: Use a word from the Word Bank to complete each sentence.

Sentence Completions

Word Bank				
broth	cloth	cost	cross	floss
frost	froth	gloss	lost	soft

1. I only use _____ tissues on my stuffy nose.

2. Does it _____ a lot to get your car fixed?

3. I _____ a dollar. It must've fallen out of my pocket.

4. You should _____ your teeth at least once a day.

5. When I woke up this morning, I saw _____ on the grass and trees.

6. I like to lick all the _____ off my milkshake before I drink it.

7. Please _____ your legs when you sit on the rug so no one trips over you.

8. We added a can of chicken _____ to Grandma's soup recipe.

9. You can use an old rag or piece of _____ to dust and polish the furniture.

10. My friend gave me bubble gum-flavored lip _____ for my birthday.

Name: _____ **Date:** _____

Directions: Use a word from the Word Bank for each section.

Word Bank				
broth	cloth	cost	cross	floss
frost	froth	gloss	lost	soft

Write a synonym for each word.

1. price _____

2. fabric _____

3. bubbles _____

4. intersect _____

Write an antonym for each word.

5. found _____

6. hard _____

7. dullness _____

Write a word that fits each category.

8. soap, shampoo, toothpaste, _____

9. soup, gravy, stew, _____

10. dew, snowflakes, raindrops, _____

Synonyms and Antonyms

Inflectional Endings

Name: _____ **Date:** _____

Directions: Study how the words change when you add new endings. Add the same endings to each word to create new words.

1. **toss**   tosses   tossing   tossed

   cross   _____   _____   _____

   floss   _____   _____   _____

   gloss   _____   _____   _____

Directions: Find three words in the Word Bank that are related to each of the spelling words. Write the words on the correct lines.

Word Bank				
clothes	softer	frosted	frosting	washcloth
softest	frosty	softness	dishcloth	

2. frost   _____   _____   _____

3. soft   _____   _____   _____

4. cloth   _____   _____   _____

Name: _____ **Date:** _____

Directions: Adjectives are words that describe a noun. Adding –y to some nouns turns them into adjectives. Add –y to each noun.

Noun	Adjective (Add –y)
boss	
frost	
point	
oil	
grouch	
cloud	

Directions: Use a word from the chart to fill in each blank.

1. Some lotions make your hands feel _____ .

2. My little brother gets very _____ if he wakes up early from his nap.

3. I could barely see through the _____ window.

4. It'll be _____ today, but it's not supposed to rain.

5. My big sister gets me so mad when she starts acting

   _____ !

6. This pencil isn't _____ enough. Can you please sharpen it for me?

Analogies

Name: _____ **Date:** _____

Directions: Use a word from the Word Bank to complete each analogy.

Word Bank				
broth	cloth	cost	cross	floss
frost	froth	gloss	lost	soft

1. **bench** is to **hard** as **couch** is to _____

2. **label** is to **size** as **price tag** is to _____

3. **find** is to **found** as **lose** is to _____

4. **Jewish** is to **Star of David** as **Christian** is to _____

5. **water** is to **ice** as **dew** is to _____

6. **color** is to **lipstick** as **shine** is to _____

7. **thick** is to **stew** as **thin** is to _____

8. **shoe** is to **leather** as **shirt** is to _____

9. **soap** is to **suds** as **milkshake** is to _____

10. **tooth surfaces** is to **toothbrush** as **between teeth** is to

    _____

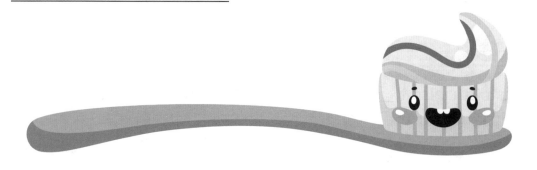

UNIT 28

/Ô/ Pattern with *au* and *aw*

- ➤ **crawl**
- ➤ **draw**
- ➤ **fault**
- ➤ **flaunt**
- ➤ **haul**
- ➤ **haunt**
- ➤ **scrawl**
- ➤ **sprawl**
- ➤ **straw**
- ➤ **vault**

Focus

This week's focus is one-syllable words that use *au* or *aw* to make the /aw/ sound and contain an initial or final blend.

Helpful Hint

A common spelling for the /aw/ sound is *aw*. The *aw* pattern appears frequently at the end of a word or syllable (*straw*, *aw·ful*). It only appears in the middle of a syllable when it precedes *k* (*hawk*), *l* (*shawl*), or *n* (*dawn*). The *au* pattern appears frequently in the middle of a syllable (*haunt*, *fault*) but never at the end.

 See page 7 for additional spelling activities.

Sentence Completions

Name: _____ **Date:** _____

Directions: Use a word from the Word Bank to complete each sentence.

Word Bank				
crawl	draw	fault	flaunt	haul
haunt	scrawl	sprawl	straw	vault

1. Sofia likes to _____ out on the carpet with her dolls.

2. I told Gramps I'd help him _____ trash to the dump this weekend.

3. I'm sorry. It's my _____ that we missed the bus.

4. The first little pig made his house out of_____ .

5. Please write more neatly. I can't read any of this

    _____ .

6. My baby cousin just learned how to _____ .

7. If we ignore this problem, it could come back to

    _____ us.

8. Most of the money is kept in a locked _____ .

9. I know your family is rich, but why do you _____ all your nice things?

10. Can you show me how to use charcoal pencil to _____ a horse?

Synonyms and Antonyms

Name: _____ **Date:** _____

Directions: Use a word from the Word Bank for each section.

Word Bank				
crawl	draw	fault	flaunt	haul
haunt	scrawl	sprawl	straw	vault

Write a synonym for each word.

1. show off _____

2. transport _____

3. spread out _____

4. bank safe _____

Write an antonym for each word.

5. strength _____

6. neat
   writing _____

Write a word that fits each category.

7. spook, scare, harass, _____

8. doodle, sketch, illustrate, _____

9. bricks, sticks, grass, _____

10. swim, fly, hop, _____

Inflectional Endings

Name: _____ **Date:** _____

Directions: Study how the words change when you add new endings. Add the same endings to each word to create new words.

1. **bawl** bawls bawling bawled

    scrawl _____ _____ _____

    sprawl _____ _____ _____

2. **taunt** taunts taunting taunted

    haunt _____ _____ _____

    flaunt _____ _____ _____

Directions: Find three words in the Word Bank that are related to each of the spelling words. Write the words on the correct lines.

Word Bank			
hauling	crawler	crawling	crawled	drawing
hauls	drew	hauled	draws	

3. draw _____ _____ _____

4. haul _____ _____ _____

5. crawl _____ _____ _____

Name: _____ **Date:** _____

Directions: Sort the words in the Word Bank into two categories: *Proper Nouns* and *Common Nouns.* Write each word in the correct column.

Word Sorts

Word Bank				
Halloween	autumn	father	Boston	Austin
frogs	Paul	August	lawn	straw

Proper Nouns	Common Nouns
○	○
○	○
○	○
○	○
○	○

Directions: Write all 10 words in ABC order.

1. _____   6. _____

2. _____   7. _____

3. _____   8. _____

4. _____   9. _____

5. _____   10. _____

Name: _____ Date: _____

Directions: Use a word from the Word Bank to complete each analogy.

Analogies

Word Bank				
crawl	draw	fault	flaunt	haul
haunt	scrawl	sprawl	straw	vault

1. **bird** is to **fly** as **lizard** is to _____

2. **soup** is to **spoon** as **milkshake** is to _____

3. **paintbrush** is to **paint** as **marker** is to _____

4. **schoolbus** is to **transport** as **moving van** is to _____

5. **angel** is to **protect** as **ghost** is to _____

6. **runner** is to **hurdle** as **gymnast** is to _____

7. **praise** is to **strength** as **blame** is to _____

8. **draw** is to **scribble** as **write** is to _____

9. **bad haircut** is to **hide** as **great haircut** is to _____

10. **in line** is to **stand** as **on the couch** is to _____

28630—180 Days of Spelling and Word Study

UNIT 29
/Ô/ Pattern with *wa* and *al*

WEEK 29

Focus

This week's focus is one-syllable words that use *wa* or *al* to make the /aw/ sound and contain an initial or final blend.

Helpful Hint

Notice that when *w* precedes *a*, it changes the short *a* sound to /ô/ (want, wash). Exceptions are *wag* (wagon) and *war* (warn).

- ➤ also
- ➤ bald
- ➤ chalk
- ➤ scald
- ➤ stalk
- ➤ swamp
- ➤ wand
- ➤ want
- ➤ wash
- ➤ watch

 See page 7 for additional spelling activities.

Name: _____ **Date:** _____

Directions: Use a word from the Word Bank to complete each sentence.

Sentence Completions

Word Bank				
also	bald	chalk	scald	stalk
swamp	wand	want	wash	watch

1. Let the soup cool so it doesn't _____ you.

2. We can draw on the driveway with my new _____ !

3. We're going to _____ the fireworks at the stadium.

4. Remember to _____ your hands with warm soap and water.

5. My best friend _____ has a birthday next month, so we're going to celebrate together.

6. We saw all kinds of creatures swimming in the _____ .

7. I _____ to be an astronaut when I grow up.

8. The tulip _____ broke in half.

9. My brother decided to shave his head, so now he's

   _____ .

10. If I had a magic _____ , I could perform all kinds of amazing tricks!

Name: _____ **Date:** _____

Directions: Use a word from the Word Bank for each section.

Word Bank				
also	bald	chalk	scald	stalk
swamp	wand	want	wash	watch

Write a synonym for each word.

1. scrub _____

2. burn _____

3. too _____

4. marsh _____

Write an antonym for each word.

5. hairy _____

6. look away _____

7. reject _____

Write a word that fits each category.

8. crayon, paint, marker, _____

9. leaf, root, flower, _____

10. black hat, cape, rabbit, _____

Word Sorts

Name: _____ **Date:**_____

Directions: Sort the words in the Word Bank into two categories: *Compound Words* and *Not Compound Words*. Write each word in the correct column.

Word Bank				
beanstalk	washcloth	flossing	chalkboard	wands
swampy	stopwatch	crosswalk	wanted	softness

Compound Words	Not Compound Words
○	○
○	○
○	○
○	○
○	○

Directions: Write all 10 words in ABC order.

1. _____ 6. _____

2. _____ 7. _____

3. _____ 8. _____

4. _____ 9. _____

5. _____ 10. _____

28630—180 Days of Spelling and Word Study

Name: _____ **Date:** _____

Directions: Answer each question in a complete sentence. Turn the question around, and use the bold word in each answer.

1. Why should we **wash** our hands before we eat?

   _____

   _____

2. If you had a magic **wand**, what would you wish for?

   _____

   _____

3. What is your favorite TV show to **watch** and why?

   _____

   _____

4. What do you **want** to be when you grow up?

   _____

   _____

5. Would you prefer to munch on a **stalk** of celery or asparagus?

   _____

   _____

6. What should you do if you **scald** your hand?

   _____

   _____

Analogies

Name: _____ **Date:** _____

Directions: Use a word from the Word Bank to complete each analogy.

Word Bank				
also	bald	chalk	scald	stalk
swamp	wand	want	wash	watch

1. **paper** is to **crayons** as **sidewalk** is to _____

2. **knight** is to **sword** as **fairy** is to _____

3. **lettuce** is to **head** as **celery** is to _____

4. **wall** is to **clock** as **wrist** is to _____

5. **broom** is to **sweep** as **sponge** is to _____

6. **lots of hair** is to **hairy** as **no hair** is to _____

7. **salmon** is to **river** as **alligator** is to _____

8. **healthy food** is to **need** as **candy bars** is to _____

9. **icy water** is to **numb** as **boiling water** is to _____

10. **either** is to **or** as **too** is to _____

UNIT 30
Schwa Sounds

Focus

This week's focus is one-syllable words that use *oo, ou,* or *u* to make the schwa sound.

Helpful Hint

All words in this list contain a schwa sound. The schwa sound is pronounced */uh/.* In this list, it is represented by *oo, ou,* or *u*.

- ➤ **brook**
- ➤ **bulb**
- ➤ **could**
- ➤ **crook**
- ➤ **gulp**
- ➤ **should**
- ➤ **skull**
- ➤ **stood**
- ➤ **sulk**
- ➤ **would**

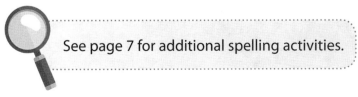

See page 7 for additional spelling activities.

Sentence Completions

Name: _____ **Date:** _____

Directions: Use a word from the Word Bank to complete each sentence.

Word Bank				
brook	bulb	could	crook	gulp
should	skull	stood	sulk	would

1. A helmet will protect your _____ if you fall and hit your head.

2. I _____ like fries with my burger.

3. We _____ in line for an hour on Black Friday.

4. A _____ stole my mom's purse right out of the shopping cart!

5. We set up our campsite in the woods, next to a small

   _____ .

6. I _____ probably start my project today instead of waiting until the last minute.

7. I dug a hole for the tulip _____ in the garden.

8. If you _____ down your food too quickly, you might get hiccups.

9. Mom told me that I needed to _____ in my room.

10. I asked if my dad _____ give me a ride to the library.

Name: _____ **Date:** _____

Directions: Use a word from the Word Bank for each section.

Word Bank				
brook	bulb	could	crook	gulp
should	skull	stood	sulk	would

Write a synonym for each word.

1. pout _____

2. swallow _____

3. thief _____

4. ought to _____

Write an antonym for each word.

5. sat down _____

6. wasn't
able to _____

7. refused _____

Write a word that fits each category.

8. collar bone, backbone, ribs, _____

9. creek, stream, river, _____

10. seed, kernel, cutting, _____

Word Sorts

Name: _____ **Date:** _____

Directions: Sort the words in the Word Bank into two categories: *Present Tense Verbs* and *Past Tense Verbs*. Write each word in the correct column.

Word Bank				
look	took	gulped	pushed	stand
shook	cook	stood	sulk	pull

Present Tense Verbs	Past Tense Verbs
○	○
○	○
○	○
○	○
○	○

Directions: Write all 10 words in ABC order.

1. _____

2. _____

3. _____

4. _____

5. _____

6. _____

7. _____

8. _____

9. _____

10. _____

Name: _____ **Date:** _____

Directions: Answer each question in a complete sentence. Turn the question around, and use the bold word in each answer.

1. Why **should** kids be allowed to choose their own bedtime?

   _____

   _____

2. How can you protect your **skull** when you skateboard?

   _____

   _____

3. Where **would** you like to travel when you grow up and why?

   _____

   _____

4. What are some reasons why children might **sulk**?

   _____

   _____

5. Why is it a bad idea to **gulp** your food?

   _____

   _____

6. Why do people like to hike along **brooks**?

   _____

   _____

Analogies

Name: _____ **Date:** _____

Directions: Use a word from the Word Bank to complete each analogy.

Word Bank				
brook	bulb	could	crook	gulp
should	skull	stood	sulk	would

1. **heart** is to **ribs** as **brain** is to _____

2. **does** is to **did** as **can** is to _____

3. **lake** is to **pond** as **river** is to _____

4. **didn't** is to **did** as **shouldn't** is to _____

5. **there** is to **their** as **wood** is to _____

6. **lie** is to **liar** as **steal** is to _____

7. **sunflower** is to **seed** as **tulip** is to _____

8. **drink** is to **chug** as **eat** is to _____

9. **sit** is to **sat** as **stand** is to _____

10. **whine** is to **complain** as **pout** is to _____

UNIT 31
Contractions

Focus

This week's focus is contractions that combine with the words *not*, *will*, *is*, or *are*.

Helpful Hint

Notice that the apostrophe acts as a bookmark, saving a spot for the missing letter or letters in a contraction. Also, remember that *i* is always capitalized in contractions that start with the word *I* (*I'm, I'll, I've*).

- ➤ can't
- ➤ didn't
- ➤ doesn't
- ➤ I'll
- ➤ it's
- ➤ they're
- ➤ wasn't
- ➤ we're
- ➤ who's
- ➤ you're

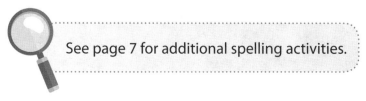

See page 7 for additional spelling activities.

Sentence Completions

Name: _____ **Date:** _____

Directions: Use a word from the Word Bank to complete each sentence.

Word Bank				
can't	didn't	doesn't	I'll	it's
they're	wasn't	we're	who's	you're

1. My brother says he _____ break my toy, but I don't believe him.

2. I _____ come to your party because I have to go on a trip.

3. I looked for my toy in the closet, but it _____ there.

4. Do you know _____ going to be the next student president?

5. My stepdad said _____ going shopping for our dresses after dinner.

6. Six plus six _____ equal ten.

7. Daniel and Aaron are coming tomorrow and _____ going to spend the night.

8. Mrs. Murphy's room is at the end of the hall. _____ show you how to get there.

9. If _____ nice on Saturday, we'll go on a picnic.

10. You look like _____ having fun on vacation!

Name: _____ **Date:** _____

Directions: Complete the chart.

Contraction	Two Words	Contraction	Missing Letters
haven't	*have not*	*haven't*	*o*
can't			
didn't			
doesn't			
I'll			
it's			
they're			
wasn't			
we're			
who's			
you're			

Homophones

Name: _____ **Date:** _____

Directions: Homophones sound the same but have different spellings and meanings. Write the correct homophone on each line.

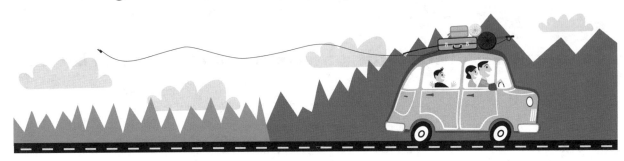

1. Is that _____ new puppy?
   (your/you're)

2. I love you because _____ always so kind to me.
   (your /you're)

3. I'm wearing a crown because _____ my birthday.
   (its/it's)

4. The turtle hid under _____ shell.
   (its/it's)

5. Please put the extra boxes over _____ .
   (there/they're)

6. My grandparents just called to tell us that _____ coming to visit tomorrow!
   (there/they're)

7. Do you know _____ coming on the field trip with us?
   (whose/who's)

8. _____ backpack is hanging in the closet?
   (Whose/Who's)

Name: _____ **Date:** _____

Directions: Answer each question in a complete sentence. Remember to turn the question around, and use the bold word in each answer.

1. Why **can't** kids drive cars?

   _____

   _____

2. Why **didn't** Cinderella stay at the ball past midnight?

   _____

   _____

3. Why **wasn't** George Washington at the first Thanksgiving?

   _____

   _____

4. Why do you think **it's** not fair to have three hours of homework every night?

   _____

   _____

5. Why **doesn't** it snow in August?

   _____

   _____

Word Sorts

Name: _____ **Date:** _____

Directions: Sort the words in the Word Bank into three categories: *Contractions with NOT, Contractions with WILL,* and *Contractions with ARE.* Write each word in the correct column.

Word Bank				
can't	they're	you're	you'll	we'll
I'll	wasn't	we're	doesn't	didn't

Contractions with NOT	Contractions with WILL	Contractions with ARE

Directions: Write all 10 words in ABC order.

1. _____   6. _____

2. _____   7. _____

3. _____   8. _____

4. _____   9. _____

5. _____   10. _____

28630—180 Days of Spelling and Word Study

UNIT 32
R-Controlled Vowels with *ar*

Focus

This week's focus is one-syllable words that contain *ar*.

Helpful Hint

Silent *e* appears at the end of words like *carve* and *starve*, but it doesn't have the usual job of making a vowel long. Instead, it's there to keep *v* company, since *v* never likes to hang out by itself at the end of a word.

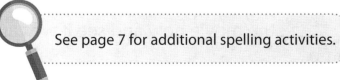

See page 7 for additional spelling activities.

WEEK 32

- ➤ carve
- ➤ charm
- ➤ march
- ➤ scarf
- ➤ shark
- ➤ sharp
- ➤ smart
- ➤ spark
- ➤ start
- ➤ starve

Sentence Completions

Name: _____ **Date:** _____

Directions: Use a word from the Word Bank to complete each sentence.

Word Bank				
carve	charm	march	scarf	shark
sharp	smart	spark	start	starve

1. My grandfather likes to _____ the turkey on Thanksgiving.

2. Molly is worried that she's going to _____ if she skips breakfast.

3. I have not seen a _____ at this beach.

4. We have a screen in front of our fireplace in case a

   _____ flies out.

5. My little brother knows how to use _____ and cuteness to get what he wants.

6. We wrapped a red _____ around the snowman.

7. This knife isn't _____ enough to cut a steak.

8. You're a _____ girl. I'm sure you'll do fine on the math test.

9. My Brownie troop is planning to _____ in the parade next weekend.

10. Let's _____ the movie now and see if we can finish it before bedtime.

28630—180 Days of Spelling and Word Study

Name: _____ **Date:** _____

Directions: Use a word from the Word Bank for each section.

Word Bank				
carve	charm	march	scarf	shark
sharp	smart	spark	start	starve

Write a synonym for each word.

1. clever _____

2. dazzle _____

3. ignite _____

4. whittle _____

Write an antonym for each word.

5. blunt _____

6. finish _____

7. eat a lot _____

Write a word that fits each category.

8. hat, boots, mittens, _____

9. walk, stroll, strut, _____

10. whale, dolphin, swordfish, _____

Inflectional Endings

Name: _____ **Date:** _____

Directions: Study how the words change when you add new endings. Add the same endings to each word to create new words.

1. **carve**   carves   carving   carved

   starve _____   _____   _____

2. **harm**   harms   harming   harmed

   charm _____   _____   _____

3. **part**   parts   parting   parted

   start _____   _____   _____

Directions: Find three words in the Word Bank that are related to each of the spelling words. Write the words on the correct lines.

Word Bank				
marches	sharpness	marched	spark plug	sparked
sharpen	sparkle	marching	sharpest	

4. spark _____   _____   _____

5. sharp _____   _____   _____

6. march _____   _____   _____

Name: _____ **Date:** _____

Directions: Sort the words in the Word Bank into two categories: *Adjectives* and *Verbs.* Write each word in the correct column.

Word Bank				
carve	smart	sharp	starve	large
start	march	hard	dark	charm

Adjectives	Verbs
○	○
○	○
○	○
○	○
○	○

Directions: Write all 10 words in ABC order.

1. _____   6. _____

2. _____   7. _____

3. _____   8. _____

4. _____   9. _____

5. _____   10. _____

Word Sorts

Analogies

Name: _____ **Date:** _____

Directions: Use a word from the Word Bank to complete each analogy.

Word Bank				
carve	charm	march	scarf	shark
sharp	smart	spark	start	starve

1. **mashed potatoes** is to **scoop** as **turkey** is to _____

2. **exercising** is to **strong** as **learning** is to _____

3. **no sleep** is to **exhaust** as **no food** is to _____

4. **peacock** is to **strut** as **band** is to _____

5. **waist** is to **belt** as **neck** is to _____

6. **old fire** is to **ember** as **new fire** is to _____

7. **spoon** is to **blunt** as **knife** is to _____

8. **necklace** is to **pendant** as **bracelet** is to _____

9. **wings** is to **eagle** as **fins** is to _____

10. **caboose** is to **end** as **engine** is to _____

UNIT 33

R-Controlled Vowels with *our*, *or*, and *ore*

WEEK 33

Focus

This week's focus is one-syllable words that contain *or*. The *our* and *ore* patterns are introduced.

Helpful Hint

Notice there are three common ways to make the /or/ sound: *our*, *ore*, and *or*. The *our* and *ore* patterns usually appear at the end of a base word or syllable *(your, core)*. The *or* pattern usually appears in the middle of a word or syllable *(port, form)*.

➤ **four**

➤ **north**

➤ **porch**

➤ **pour**

➤ **score**

➤ **short**

➤ **sport**

➤ **store**

➤ **storm**

➤ **tour**

See page 7 for additional spelling activities.

Name: _____ **Date:**_____

Sentence Completions

Directions: Use a word from the Word Bank to complete each sentence.

Word Bank				
four	north	porch	pour	score
short	sport	store	storm	tour

1. We stopped at the _____ to buy more milk and eggs.

2. Tennis is my favorite _____ to play.

3. Since our house faces _____ , we don't get a lot of morning sun.

4. Have you ever been on a _____ of the White House?

5. There are _____ suits in a deck of cards: hearts, clubs, diamonds, and spades.

6. Don't _____ too much dressing on your salad.

7. I've been growing so much! Now, all my pants are too

    _____ .

8. What was the final _____ of the baseball game?

9. We better get back before the _____ comes.

10. This hanging basket of flowers will look so nice on the front

    _____ !

Name: _____ **Date:**_____

Directions: Use a word from the Word Bank for each section.

Word Bank				
four	north	porch	pour	score
short	sports	store	storm	tour

Write a synonym for each word.

1. market _____

2. athletics_____

3. explore _____

4. blizzard _____

Write an antonym for each word.

5. tall _____

6. south _____

Write a word that fits each category.

7. patio, deck, terrace, _____

8. six, eight, two, _____

9. spill, gush, ooze, _____

10. rating, grade, mark, _____

Synonyms and Antonyms

205

Prefixes and Suffixes

Name: _____ **Date:**_____

Directions: Adjectives are words that describe a noun. If you add –y to some nouns, they turn into adjectives. Add –y to each noun.

Noun	Adjective (Add –y)
storm	
sport	
thorn	
bulk	
mush	
push	

Directions: Use a word from the chart to fill in each blank.

1. I got scratched when I grabbed my ball from under the

   _____ rosebushes.

2. The sky looks _____ . I think it's going to rain soon.

3. Don't be so _____ . I'll talk to Ellie when I'm ready.

4. Mom bought me a pair of _____ sandals for summer camp.

5. I didn't eat my cereal fast enough, and it got all _____ .

6. The art project is too _____ to fit in my backpack.

Name: _____ **Date:** _____

Directions: Answer each question in a complete sentence. Turn the question around, and use the bold word in each answer.

1. What usually happens to the weather when you travel **north**?

   _____

   _____

2. Why do people like to sit on their **porches**?

   _____

   _____

3. What is your favorite **sport** to play and why?

   _____

   _____

4. Why should you be careful when you **pour** a drink?

   _____

   _____

5. What can you do to stay safe during a thunder**storm**?

   _____

   _____

6. Why do people **tour** historic homes?

   _____

   _____

Analogies

Name: _____ **Date:** _____

Directions: Use a word from the Word Bank to complete each analogy.

Word Bank				
four	north	porch	pour	score
short	sport	store	storm	tour

1. **eat** is to **restaurant** as **shop** is to _____

2. **triangle** is to **three** as **rectangle** is to _____

3. **tidal wave** is to **flood** as **hurricane** is to _____

4. **back of house** is to **deck** as **front of house** is to _____

5. **checkers** is to **game** as **hockey** is to _____

6. **Antarctica** is to **south** as **Arctic Circle** is to _____

7. **second inning** is to **time** as **4 to 3** is to _____

8. **sugar** is to **sprinkle** as **milk** is to _____

9. **hiking trail** is to **explore** as **museum** is to _____

10. **giraffe** is to **tall** as **mouse** is to _____

UNIT 34

R-Controlled Vowels with *ir*

- birth
- chirp
- first
- shirt
- squirm
- squirt
- stir
- third
- thirst
- twirl

Focus

This week's focus is one-syllable words that contain *ir* and an initial or final blend.

Helpful Hint

The *ir* pattern always says /er/ unless it is followed by a silent *e (wire, fire)* or is preceded by a vowel other than *u (hair, their)*.

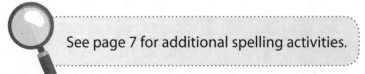

See page 7 for additional spelling activities.

Name: _____ **Date:** _____

Directions: Use a word from the Word Bank to complete each sentence.

Word Bank				
birth	chirp	first	shirt	squirm
squirt	stir	third	thirst	twirl

1. My dad always wears a _____ and tie to work.

2. I love listening to the birds _____ at the feeder in my backyard.

3. Just add a _____ of food coloring to the frosting.

4. This icy glass of lemonade will quench your _____ .

5. In _____ grade, we'll learn how to multiply bigger numbers.

6. Make sure you _____ the sauce so it doesn't burn.

7. I always _____ in my seat during assemblies.

8. Dad wasn't at the _____ of my baby brother because he was overseas.

9. Chelsea is teaching me how to _____ a baton.

10. Make sure everyone gets a slice _____ before you go back for seconds.

Name: _____ **Date:** _____

Directions: Use a word from the Word Bank for each section.

Word Bank				
birth	chirp	first	shirt	squirm
squirt	stir	third	thirst	twirl

Write a synonym for each word.

1. spin _____

2. wiggle _____

3. mix _____

4. burst _____

Write an antonym for each word.

5. death _____

6. last _____

Write a word that fits each category.

7. pants, socks, shoes, _____

8. tweet, quack, cluck, _____

9. fifth, first, second, _____

10. hunger, coldness, tiredness, _____

Inflectional Endings

Name: _____   **Date:** _____

Directions: Study how the words change when you add new endings. Add the same endings to each word to create new words.

1. **swirl**   swirls   swirling   swirled

   twirl   _____   _____   _____

2. **skirt**   skirts   skirting   skirted

   squirt   _____   _____   _____

3. **firm**   firms   firming   firmed

   squirm   _____   _____   _____

Directions: Find three words in the Word Bank that are related to each of the spelling words. Write the words on the correct lines.

Word Bank				
thirsty	birthday	stirring	thirsts	childbirth
stirred	thirsted	stirs	births	

4. stir   _____   _____   _____

5. birth   _____   _____   _____

6. thirst   _____   _____   _____

Name: _____ **Date:** _____

Directions: Add –*ing* and –*ed* to the words. Remember to double the *r*.

Verb	Add –*ing*	Add –*ed*
stir		
star		
scar		
slur		
spur		

Directions: Use a word from the chart to fill in each blank.

1. Keep _____ the chocolate chips until they're completely melted.

2. Lily was so tired that she started babbling and _____ her words.

3. My sister's arm is _____ from all the burns she got in the kitchen.

4. Is that the same actor who _____ in the movie we saw last week?

5. All of this bitterly cold weather is _____ people to plan trips to Florida.

When a one-syllable verb ends with a single vowel followed by one consonant, double the consonant before adding a vowel suffix such as –*ed*, –*ing*, or –*y*.

Analogies

Name: _____ **Date:** _____

Directions: Use a word from the Word Bank to complete each analogy.

Word Bank				
birth	chirp	first	shirt	squirm
squirt	stir	third	thirst	twirl

1. **caboose** is to **last** as **engine** is to _____

2. **egg** is to **hatch** as **mammal** is to _____

3. **water** is to **pour** as **ketchup** is to _____

4. **gold** is to **first** as **bronze** is to _____

5. **duck** is to **quack** as **robin** is to _____

6. **waist** is to **pants** as **collar** is to _____

7. **knife** is to **cut** as **spoon** is to _____

8. **food** is to **hunger** as **drink** is to _____

9. **gymnast** is to **flip** as **dancer** is to _____

10. **tired** is to **stretch** as **restless** is to _____

UNIT 35

R-Controlled Vowels
with *er* and *ur*

WEEK 35

- blurb
- blurt
- burst
- church
- clerk
- germs
- perch
- slurp
- stern
- were

Focus

This week's focus is one-syllable words that contain *er* or *ur*.

Helpful Hint

The *ur* pattern always says /er/ unless it's preceded by *a* or *o (your, aura)*. The *er* pattern always says /er/ unless it's preceded by *e (deer)* or followed by *e (here, there)*.

 See page 7 for additional spelling activities.

Sentence Completions

Name: _____ **Date:** _____

Directions: Use a word from the Word Bank to complete each sentence.

Word Bank				
blurb	blurt	burst	church	clerk
germs	perch	slurp	stern	were

1. Blue jays like to _____ on branches in my yard.

2. Even though my grandpa has a _____ look on his face, he's very nice.

3. Read the _____ on the back of the book to see if it sounds interesting.

4. We went to town hall and paid the _____ for our dog license.

5. Don't _____ out the answer before everyone has a chance to solve the math problem.

6. We went to _____ on Sunday morning.

7. I used my straw to _____ up every bit of the chocolate milkshake.

8. If you fill the balloon up too much, it'll _____ .

9. My neighbor's great-grandparents _____ on a trip last week.

10. Wash your hands so you don't spread _____ .

Name: _____ **Date:** _____

Directions: Use a word from the Word Bank for each section.

Synonyms and Antonyms

Word Bank				
blurb	blurt	burst	church	clerk
germs	perch	slurp	stern	were

Write a synonym for each word.

1. explode _____

2. sales person _____

3. summary_____

4. roost _____

Write an antonym for each word.

5. friendly _____

6. will be _____

7. stay quiet _____

Write a word that fits each category.

8. temple, mosque, chapel, _____

9. guzzle, drink, sip, _____

10. viruses, diseases, bugs, _____

Name: _____ **Date:** _____

Directions: Sort the words in the Word Bank into two categories: *Verbs* and *Adverbs*. Write each word in the correct column.

Word Bank				
sternly	firmly	squirm	burst	softly
partly	slurp	chirp	hardly	blurt

Verbs	Adverbs
○	○
○	○
○	○
○	○
○	○

Directions: Write all 10 words in ABC order.

1. _____   6. _____

2. _____   7. _____

3. _____   8. _____

4. _____   9. _____

5. _____   10. _____

Name: _____ **Date:** _____

Directions: Sometimes you can change a verb to a noun by adding the suffix –er to the end. Add –er to each verb.

Verb	Noun (Add –er)
teach	
play	
read	
lead	
farm	
build	

Directions: Use a word from the chart to fill in each blank.

1. A person who takes care of plants and animals on a farm:

   _____

2. A person who teaches children how to read, write, and do math:

   _____

3. A person who uses tools to build houses: _____

4. A person who enjoys reading books: _____

5. A person who plays on a team: _____

6. A person who takes charge and leads others: _____

Name: _____ **Date:** _____

Directions: Use a word from the Word Bank to complete each analogy.

Analogies

Word Bank				
blurb	blurt	burst	church	clerk
germs	perch	slurp	stern	were

1. **eat** is to **restaurant** as **pray** is to _____

2. **firecracker** is to **explode** as **water balloon** is to _____

3. **person** is to **chair** as **bird** is to _____

4. **healthy** is to **vitamins** as **sick** is to _____

5. **quiet** is to **sip** as **loud** is to _____

6. **restaurant** is to **waiter** as **store** is to _____

7. **is** is to **are** as **was** is to _____

8. **front of book** is to **title** as **back of book** is to _____

9. **"Here you go"** is to **friendly** as **"Don't touch!"** is to _____

10. **raise your hand** is to **wait** as **don't raise your hand** is to

_____

UNIT 36
–Y Endings

WEEK 36

Focus

This week's focus is two-syllable words that start with a closed syllable and end with *y*.

Helpful Hint

All of the words on this list have two syllables. The first syllable is closed, which means it ends with a short vowel plus a consonant. The syllables are divided between the consonants (*hap·py, twen·ty*). Notice that *y* makes a long *e* sound at the end of a two-syllable word when the second syllable is unstressed.

- candy
- funny
- happy
- jelly
- penny
- pretty
- puppy
- silly
- twenty
- ugly

See page 7 for additional spelling activities.

Name: _____ **Date:** _____

Directions: Use a word from the Word Bank to complete each sentence.

Sentence Completions

Word Bank				
candy	funny	happy	jelly	penny
pretty	puppy	silly	twenty	ugly

1. I found _____ dollars in my back pocket!

2. We were so _____ when we got home after a long day.

3. Would you like grape _____ on your toast?

4. The girls look so _____ in their summer dresses.

5. I only have two nickels and a _____ left in my piggy bank.

6. How do you train your _____ to fetch a ball?

7. My friend told me a _____ joke at lunch yesterday.

8. Dad looked so _____ when we dressed him up for our tea party!

9. Our goody bags were full of stickers, pencils, and

   _____ .

10. That shirt is so _____ . Who would ever wear it?

Name: _____ **Date:** _____

Directions: Use a word from the Word Bank for each section.

Word Bank				
candy	funny	happy	jelly	penny
pretty	puppy	silly	twenty	ugly

Write a synonym for each word.

1. amusing _____

2. beautiful _____

3. sweets _____

Write an antonym for each word.

4. sad _____

5. serious _____

6. attractive _____

Write a word that fits each category.

7. nickel, dime, quarter, _____

8. butter, honey, cream cheese, _____

9. forty, ninety, eighty, _____

10. kitten, lamb, calf, _____

Name: _____ **Date:** _____

Directions: Plural means more than one. Write each singular noun as a plural noun. Change the *y* to *i*, then add *–es*.

Singular Noun	Plural Noun
puppy	
penny	
candy	
bunny	
jelly	

Directions: The *–er* suffix means *more*, and *–est* means *most*. Add each suffix to the words in the chart. Change the *y* to *i* before adding the suffixes.

Adjective	More	Most
ugly		
pretty		
funny		
silly		
sloppy		

Name: _____ **Date:** _____

Directions: Answer each question in a complete sentence. Turn the question around, and use the bold word in each answer.

1. Where will you live in **twenty** years?

   _____

   _____

2. Why do most children like **candy**?

   _____

   _____

3. Why is it hard work to take care of a **puppy**?

   _____

   _____

4. What makes you **happy**?

   _____

   _____

5. Why do you think people should save **pennies**?

   _____

   _____

6. What makes someone **funny**?

   _____

   _____

Analogies

Name: _____ **Date:** _____

Directions: Use a word from the Word Bank to complete each analogy.

Word Bank				
candy	funny	happy	jelly	penny
pretty	puppy	silly	twenty	ugly

1. **frown** is to **sad** as **smile** is to _____

2. **cat** is to **kitten** as **dog** is to _____

3. **5 tens** is to **fifty** as **2 tens** is to _____

4. **cola** is to **soda** as **chocolate** is to _____

5. **25¢** is to **quarter** as **1¢** is to _____

6. **judge** is to **serious** as **comedian** is to _____

7. **salt** is to **pepper** as **peanut butter** is to _____

8. **boy** is to **handsome** as **girl** is to _____

9. **flowers** is to **beautiful** as **mold** is to _____

10. **lion tamer** is to **brave** as **clown** is to _____

Answer Key

Week 1 Day 1 (page 12)

1.	last	6.	ask
2.	fact	7.	mask
3.	blast	8.	clasp
4.	task	9.	past
5.	cast	10.	fast

Week 1 Day 2 (page 13)

1.	task	6.	last
2.	blast	7.	past
3.	fact	8.	cast
4.	fast	9.	clasp
5.	ask	10.	mask

Week 1 Day 3 (page 14)

Responses should be phrased as the correct sentence types.

Week 1 Day 4 (page 15)

1. asks, asking, asked
2. lasts, lasting, lasted
3. clasps, clasping, clasped
4. faster, fastest, fastball
5. masking, unmask, masks
6. blasted, blasting, blast off

Week 1 Day 5 (page 16)

1.	mask	6.	blast
2.	fast	7.	task
3.	past	8.	last
4.	clasp	9.	ask
5.	cast	10.	fact

Week 2 Day 1 (page 18)

1.	land	6.	pants
2.	lamp	7.	slant
3.	bland	8.	damp
4.	stamp	9.	stand
5.	hand	10.	plant

Week 2 Day 2 (page 19)

1.	slants	6.	plant
2.	stamp	7.	land
3.	damp	8.	pants
4.	bland	9.	hand
5.	stand	10.	lamp

Week 2 Day 3 (page 20)

Responses should be phrased as the correct sentence types.

Week 2 Day 4 (page 21)

1. plants, planting, planted
2. stamps, stamping, stamped
3. lands, landing, landed
4. handshake, handful, handy
5. standby, standing, kickstand
6. lampshade, lamps, streetlamp

Week 2 Day 5 (page 22)

1.	lamp	6.	bland
2.	land	7.	pants
3.	damp	8.	plant
4.	stand	9.	stamp
5.	hand	10.	slant

Week 3 Day 1 (page 24)

1.	list	6.	milk
2.	gift	7.	risk
3.	mist	8.	quilt
4.	twist	9.	hint
5.	squint	10.	lift

Week 3 Day 2 (page 25)

1.	mist	6.	squint
2.	hint	7.	twist
3.	gift	8.	quilt
4.	risk	9.	milk
5.	lift	10.	list

Week 3 Day 3 (page 26)

Responses should be phrased as the correct sentence types.

Week 3 Day 4 (page 27)

1. squints, squinting, squinted
2. lifts, lifting, lifted
3. twists, twisting, twisted
4. gifted, gifts, gift wrap
5. risky, risked, riskier
6. quilts, quilting, quilted

Week 3 Day 5 (page 28)

1.	milk	6.	hint
2.	squint	7.	lift
3.	quilt	8.	risk
4.	gift	9.	list
5.	mist	10.	twist

Week 4 Day 1 (page 30)

1.	next	6.	slept
2.	desk	7.	went
3.	blend	8.	spend
4.	help	9.	felt
5.	best	10.	left

Week 4 Day 2 (page 31)

1.	blend	6.	best
2.	slept	7.	left
3.	help	8.	next
4.	felt	9.	desk
5.	went	10.	spend

Week 4 Day 3 (page 32)

Past Tense Verbs (first chart): rested, asked, planted, twisted, helped

Past Tense Verbs (second chart): slept, kept, felt, left, went

Week 4 Day 4 (page 33)

1. spends, spending, spent
   bends, bending, bent
2. sleeps, sleeping, slept
   keeps, keeping, kept
3. blender, blended, blending
4. helping, helpful, helped
5. leaving, leave, leaves

Answer Key *(cont.)*

Week 4 Day 5 (page 34)

1.	desk	6.	slept
2.	best	7.	spend
3.	left	8.	felt
4.	blend	9.	help
5.	went	10.	next

Week 5 Day 1 (page 36)

1.	jump	6.	stomp
2.	dusk	7.	must
3.	fond	8.	blunt
4.	just	9.	stump
5.	pond	10.	does

Week 5 Day 2 (page 37)

1.	fond	6.	stomp
2.	must	7.	dusk
3.	just	8.	jump
4.	pond	9.	stump
5.	blunt	10.	does

Week 5 Day 3 (page 38)

Responses should be phrased as the correct sentence types.

Week 5 Day 4 (page 39)

Present Tense Verbs: dump, rust, pump, bunt, stop
Past Tense Verbs: jumped, dusted, stomped, hunted, bumped
ABC Order: bumped, bunt, dump, dusted, hunted, jumped, pump, rust, stomped, stop

Week 5 Day 5 (page 40)

1.	dusk	6.	stomp
2.	pond	7.	blunt
3.	just	8.	does
4.	fond	9.	jump
5.	stump	10.	must

Week 6 Day 1 (page 42)

1.	smock	6.	clock
2.	stack	7.	click
3.	pluck	8.	snack
4.	speck	9.	flock
5.	black	10.	stick

Week 6 Day 2 (page 43)

1.	stack	6.	snack
2.	smock	7.	speck
3.	pluck	8.	flock
4.	black	9.	click
5.	stick	10.	clock

Week 6 Day 3 (page 44)

–ing: clicking, snacking, picking, stacking, blocking
–ed: clicked, snacked, picked, stacked, blocked

1. stacking
2. picked
3. blocking
4. snacked
5. clicked

Week 6 Day 4 (page 45)

1. clicks, clicking, clicked
2. stacks, stacking, stacked
3. plucks, plucking, plucked
4. stuck, sticky, sticking
5. blacksmith, blacken, blackest
6. clockwise, clocks, clockwork

Week 6 Day 5 (page 46)

1.	black	6.	speck
2.	stick	7.	smock
3.	flock	8.	pluck
4.	stack	9.	clock
5.	click	10.	snack

Week 7 Day 1 (page 48)

1.	numb	6.	knelt
2.	knit	7.	wreck
3.	knock	8.	knob
4.	knot	9.	wrist
5.	lamb	10.	wrap

Week 7 Day 2 (page 49)

1.	lamb	6.	wrap
2.	knock	7.	knelt
3.	knob	8.	wrist
4.	numb	9.	knit
5.	wreck	10.	knot

Week 7 Day 3 (page 50)

Responses should be phrased as the correct sentence types.

Week 7 Day 4 (page 51)

1. kneels, kneeling, knelt
2. knots, knotting, knotted
3. wrecks, wrecking, wrecked
4. unwrap, wrapper, wrapping
5. knitting, knitter, knits
6. doorknob, knobby, knobs

Week 7 Day 5 (page 52)

1.	knock	6.	knit
2.	knelt	7.	wreck
3.	wrist	8.	knob
4.	lamb	9.	knot
5.	wrap	10.	numb

Week 8 Day 1 (page 54)

1.	plate	6.	snake
2.	write	7.	skate
3.	slide	8.	state
4.	flake	9.	knife
5.	stale	10.	smile

Week 8 Day 2 (page 55)

1.	plate	6.	write
2.	knife	7.	slide
3.	flake	8.	snake
4.	smile	9.	state
5.	stale	10.	skate

Week 8 Day 3 (page 56)

–ing: skating, flaking, smiling, stating, blaming
–ed: skated, flaked, smiled, stated, blamed
Past Tense Verbs: slid, wrote, took, made, bit

Week 8 Day 4 (page 57)

1. skates, skating, skated
2. smiles, smiling, smiled
3. flakes, flaking, flaked
4. wrote, writer, writing
5. sliding, slid, slides
6. snakeskin, rattlesnake, snakes

Answer Key *(cont.)*

Week 8 Day 5 (page 58)

1. slide
2. snake
3. stale
4. state
5. knife
6. flake
7. smile
8. skate
9. write
10. plate

Week 9 Day 1 (page 60)

1. spoke
2. close
3. globe
4. wrote
5. stove
6. flute
7. plume
8. slope
9. smoke
10. stone

Week 9 Day 2 (page 61)

1. globe
2. stove
3. slope
4. plume
5. close
6. spoke
7. wrote
8. flute
9. smoke
10. stone

Week 9 Day 3 (page 62)

–ing: smoking, sloping, hoping, voting, closing
–ed: smoked, sloped, hoped, voted, closed
Past Tense Verbs: spoke, stole, wrote, froze, woke

Week 9 Day 4 (page 63)

Sentences should include bold words.

Week 9 Day 5 (page 64)

1. flute
2. smoke
3. plume
4. globe
5. stove
6. slope
7. spoke
8. close
9. stone
10. wrote

Week 10 Day 1 (page 66)

1. crisp
2. grade
3. truck
4. stripe
5. drive
6. brand
7. crust
8. scrape
9. bride
10. sprint

Week 10 Day 2 (page 67)

1. scrape
2. grade
3. drive
4. crust
5. bride
6. crisp
7. sprint
8. truck
9. stripe
10. brand

Week 10 Day 3 (page 68)

Short Vowel Words: brand, crisp, crust, sprint, truck
Long Vowel Words: bride, drive, grade, scrape, stripe
ABC Order: brand, bride, crisp, crust, drive, grade, scrape, sprint, stripe, truck

Week 10 Day 4 (page 69)

1. grades, grading, graded
2. sprints, sprinting, sprinted
3. scrapes, scraping, scraped
4. driver, drove, driving
5. crispy, crispier, crispiest
6. trucks, truckload, trucker

Week 10 Day 5 (page 70)

1. crust
2. grade
3. drive
4. bride
5. crisp
6. sprint
7. truck
8. stripe
9. brand
10. scrape

Week 11 Day 1 (page 72)

1. splash
2. branch
3. thumb
4. shelf
5. lunch
6. quench
7. shrimp
8. fresh
9. throne
10. crash

Week 11 Day 2 (page 73)

1. splash
2. branch
3. shelf
4. lunch
5. fresh
6. quench
7. crash
8. throne
9. shrimp
10. thumb

Week 11 Day 3 (page 74)

Plural Nouns (first chart): benches, brushes, lunches, flashes, punches
Plural Nouns (second chart): shelves, elves, halves, calves, wives

Week 11 Day 4 (page 75)

1. splashes, splashing, splashed
2. crunches, crunching, crunched
3. quenches, quenching, quenched
4. thumbtack, thumbnail, thumbs
5. lunches, lunchroom, lunchtime
6. fresher, freshly, freshness

Week 11 Day 5 (page 76)

1. splash
2. thumb
3. branch
4. throne
5. shrimp
6. lunch
7. shelf
8. crash
9. quench
10. fresh

Week 12 Day 1 (page 78)

1. price
2. spruce
3. brace
4. cell
5. place
6. slice
7. cent
8. gem
9. stage
10. spice

Week 12 Day 2 (page 79)

Short Vowel Words: since, gem, cent, cell, gel
Long Vowel Words: price, place, stage, spice, slice
ABC Order: cell, cent, gel, gem, place, price, since, slice, spice, stage

Week 12 Day 3 (page 80)

Sentences should include bold words.

Week 12 Day 4 (page 81)

1. slices, slicing, sliced
2. places, placing, placed
3. stages, staging, staged
4. spicy, spices, spiced
5. priceless, pricey, overpriced
6. cells, cellular, cell phone

Answer Key (cont.)

Week 12 Day 5 (page 82)

1. brace
2. spice
3. cent
4. stage
5. place
6. cell
7. gem
8. slice
9. price
10. spruce

Week 13 Day 1 (page 84)

1. skunk
2. blink
3. drink
4. trunk
5. string
6. thank
7. wrong
8. bring
9. chunk
10. think

Week 13 Day 2 (page 85)

1. chunk
2. drink
3. think
4. blink
5. wrong
6. trunk
7. bring
8. string
9. skunk
10. thank

Week 13 Day 3 (page 86)

1. drinks, drinking, drank
2. blinks, blinking, blinked
3. thanks, thanking, thanked
4. brings, bringing, brought
5. thinks, thinking, thought
6. drawstring, stringy, strings

Week 13 Day 4 (page 87)

Past Tense (first chart): thanked, blinked, banged, dunked, honked
Past Tense (second chart): thought, brought, drank, sang, sank

Week 13 Day 5 (page 88)

1. skunk
2. string
3. think
4. trunk
5. drink
6. wrong
7. blink
8. bring
9. thank
10. chunk

Week 14 Day 1 (page 90)

1. stray
2. tray
3. away
4. gray
5. fray
6. clay
7. spray
8. stay
9. pray
10. play

Week 14 Day 2 (page 91)

1. fray
2. stray
3. pray
4. away
5. play
6. stay
7. gray
8. spray
9. clay
10. tray

Week 14 Day 3 (page 92)

1. sprays, spraying, sprayed
   prays, praying, prayed
   strays, straying, strayed
   frays, fraying, frayed
2. grayish, grayer, grayest
3. player, playful, playing
4. overstay, staying, stayed

Week 14 Day 4 (page 93)

Sentences should include bold words.

Week 14 Day 5 (page 94)

1. gray
2. spray
3. play
4. away
5. clay
6. fray
7. tray
8. stay
9. pray
10. stray

Week 15 Day 1 (page 96)

1. brain
2. chair
3. trail
4. train
5. plain
6. waist
7. grain
8. paint
9. frail
10. sprain

Week 15 Day 2 (page 97)

1. sprain
2. trail
3. waist
4. paint
5. plain
6. frail
7. train
8. chair
9. grain
10. brain

Week 15 Day 3 (page 98)

Singular Nouns: brain, chain, train, waist, paint
Plural Nouns: chairs, trails, grains, snails, braids
ABC Order: braids, brain, chain, chairs, grains, paint, snails, trails, train, waist

Week 15 Day 4 (page 99)

Sentences should include the bold words.

Week 15 Day 5 (page 100)

1. chair
2. paint
3. waist
4. grain
5. train
6. sprain
7. brain
8. trail
9. frail
10. plain

Week 16 Day 1 (page 102)

1. dream
2. wreath
3. feast
4. knead
5. clean
6. speak
7. stream
8. clear
9. cheap
10. scream

Week 16 Day 2 (page 103)

1. speak
2. clear
3. feast
4. dream
5. cheap
6. scream
7. clean
8. wreath
9. knead
10. stream

Week 16 Day 3 (page 104)

1. cleans, cleaning, cleaned
2. dreams, dreaming, dreamed
3. kneads, kneading, kneaded
4. cheaper, cheapest, cheaply
5. spoke, speaking, speaker
6. clearly, clearing, cleared

Week 16 Day 4 (page 105)

Plural Nouns (first chart): beaches, peaches, leashes, speeches, screeches
Plural Nouns (second chart): feet, teeth, sheep, deer, people

Answer Key (cont.)

Week 16 Day 5 (page 106)

1. clean
2. cheap
3. knead
4. stream
5. dream
6. feast
7. wreath
8. clear
9. scream
10. speak

Week 17 Day 1 (page 108)

1. three
2. street
3. sheet
4. screen
5. green
6. teeth
7. speech
8. bleed
9. sleep
10. kneel

Week 17 Day 2 (page 109)

1. teeth
2. street
3. sheet
4. screen
5. sleep
6. bleed
7. green
8. three
9. kneel
10. speech

Week 17 Day 3 (page 110)

1. see
2. beat
3. week
4. need
5. heal
6. meet
7. deer
8. steal
9. seams
10. bee

Week 17 Day 4 (page 111)

Sentences should include bold words.

Week 17 Day 5 (page 112)

1. teeth
2. green
3. kneel
4. three
5. sheet
6. sleep
7. street
8. screen
9. speech
10. bleed

Week 18 Day 1 (page 114)

1. slight
2. grind
3. child
4. flight
5. find
6. blind
7. knight
8. mighty
9. fright
10. bright

Week 18 Day 2 (page 115)

1. knight
2. grind
3. mighty
4. fright
5. blind
6. slight
7. find
8. bright
9. flight
10. child

Week 18 Day 3 (page 116)

–er: higher, lighter, tighter, brighter, milder, kinder
–est: highest, lightest, tightest, brightest, mildest, kindest

1. tighter
2. kindest
3. brighter
4. milder
5. highest

Week 18 Day 4 (page 117)

Adjectives: slight, bright, mighty, blind, kind
Nouns: nightlight, child, thigh, knight, flight
ABC Order: blind, bright, child, flight, kind, knight, mighty, nightlight, slight, thigh

Week 18 Day 5 (page 118)

1. grind
2. knight
3. fright
4. flight
5. bright
6. child
7. mighty
8. slight
9. blind
10. find

Week 19 Day 1 (page 120)

1. roast
2. float
3. groan
4. boast
5. throat
6. oath
7. coach
8. croak
9. toast
10. coast

Week 19 Day 2 (page 121)

1. boast
2. oath
3. coast
4. float
5. coach
6. groan
7. croak
8. toast
9. throat
10. roast

Week 19 Day 3 (page 122)

1. coaches, coaching, coached
2. groans, groaning, groaned
3. boasts, boasting, boasted
4. afloat, floating, floaty
5. roasted, roaster, roasting
6. toaster, toasted, toasty

Week 19 Day 4 (page 123)

Sentences should include bold words.

Week 19 Day 5 (page 124)

1. croak
2. coach
3. throat
4. toast
5. groan
6. coast
7. oath
8. float
9. roast
10. boast

Week 20 Day 1 (page 126)

1. throw
2. glow
3. own
4. know
5. snow
6. blow
7. flow
8. grow
9. stow
10. slow

Week 20 Day 2 (page 127)

1. throw
2. stow
3. glow
4. own
5. grow
6. slow
7. snow
8. blow
9. know
10. flow

Week 20 Day 3 (page 128)

1. grows, growing, grew
   knows, knowing, knew
   throws, throwing, threw
2. shows, showing, showed
   flows, flowing, flowed
3. owner, owned, owns
4. knowledge, known, unknown
5. snowball, snowflake, snowfall

Answer Key (cont.)

Week 20 Day 4 (page 129)

Present Tense Verbs: own, flow, glow, throw, stow
Past Tense Verbs: blew, snowed, grew, knew, showed
ABC Order: blew, flow, glow, grew, knew, own, showed, snowed, stow, throw

Week 20 Day 5 (page 130)

1. snow
2. slow
3. throw
4. blow
5. flow
6. glow
7. own
8. stow
9. know
10. grow

Week 21 Day 1 (page 132)

1. post
2. fold
3. bolt
4. hold
5. both
6. sold
7. mold
8. cold
9. told
10. most

Week 21 Day 2 (page 133)

1. most
2. fold
3. told
4. hold
5. both
6. cold
7. sold
8. bolt
9. mold
10. post

Week 21 Day 3 (page 134)

1. tells, telling, told
2. posts, posting, posted
3. folds, folding, folded
4. held, holding, holder
5. colder, coldest, coldness
6. combs, combing, honeycomb

Week 21 Day 4 (page 135)

Adverbs: coldly, boldy, slowly, kindly, lightly, shyly
1. kindly
2. lightly
3. shyly
4. boldly
5. slowly

Week 21 Day 5 (page 136)

1. cold
2. mold
3. fold
4. post
5. sold
6. told
7. most
8. bolt
9. both
10. hold

Week 22 Day 1 (page 138)

1. tooth
2. spoon
3. bloom
4. school
5. droop
6. broom
7. scoop
8. groom
9. booth
10. smooth

Week 22 Day 2 (page 139)

1. droop
2. bloom
3. booth
4. scoop
5. smooth
6. groom
7. spoon
8. tooth
9. broom
10. school

Week 22 Day 3 (page 140)

1. scoops, scooping, scooped
   droops, drooping, drooped
2. blooms, blooming, bloomed
   grooms, grooming, groomed
3. teaspoon, tablespoon, spoonful
4. toothbrush, toothpaste, teeth
5. preschool, schoolhouse, schoolwork

Week 22 Day 4 (page 141)

Sentences should include bold words.

Week 22 Day 5 (page 142)

1. school
2. scoop
3. spoon
4. tooth
5. groom
6. booth
7. broom
8. droop
9. smooth
10. bloom

Week 23 Day 1 (page 144)

1. grew
2. knew
3. screw
4. threw
5. crew
6. true
7. drew
8. fruit
9. blew
10. suit

Week 23 Day 2 (page 145)

1. crew
2. drew
3. suit
4. true
5. threw
6. grew
7. knew
8. fruit
9. screw
10. blew

Week 23 Day 3 (page 146)

Present Tense Verbs: blow, know, bloom, grow, droop
Past Tense Verbs: glued, drew, flew, threw, chewed
ABC Order: bloom, blow, chewed, drew, droop, flew, glued, grow, know, threw

Week 23 Day 4 (page 147)

Sentences should include bold words.

Week 23 Day 5 (page 148)

1. screw
2. fruit
3. suit
4. blew
5. crew
6. grew
7. threw
8. drew
9. knew
10. true

Week 24 Day 1 (page 150)

1. proud
2. flour
3. ground
4. around
5. crouch
6. found
7. count
8. cloud
9. sprout
10. sound

Week 24 Day 2 (page 151)

1. sound
2. sprout
3. crouch
4. count
5. found
6. proud
7. ground
8. around
9. flour
10. cloud

Answer Key (cont.)

Week 24 Day 3 (page 152)

1. grinds, grinding, ground
   finds, finding, found
2. counts, counting, counted
3. sprouts, sprouting, sprouted
4. proudly, prouder, proudest
5. cloudy, clouds, cloudless
6. crouches, crouching, crouched

Week 24 Day 4 (page 153)

Adverbs: loudly, proudly, rudely, smoothly, gladly, sadly

1. rudely
2. sadly
3. gladly
4. loudly
5. proudly
6. smoothly

Week 24 Day 5 (page 154)

1. found
2. sprout
3. count
4. cloud
5. flour
6. around
7. ground
8. proud
9. sound
10. crouch

Week 25 Day 1 (page 156)

1. clown
2. powder
3. flower
4. scowl
5. crown
6. growl
7. crowd
8. drown
9. prowl
10. plow

Week 25 Day 2 (page 157)

1. crowd
2. prowl
3. scowl
4. crown
5. drown
6. growl
7. clown
8. powder
9. plow
10. flower

Week 25 Day 3 (page 158)

1. drowns, drowning, drowned
2. scowls, scowling, scowled
   growls, growling, growled
   prowls, prowling, prowled
3. powdery, powdered, powders
4. flowery, sunflower, flowerpot
5. crowded, overcrowding, crowds

Week 25 Day 4 (page 159)

Sentences should include bold words.

Week 25 Day 5 (page 160)

1. powder
2. flower
3. crown
4. clown
5. plow
6. drown
7. growl
8. scowl
9. prowl
10. crowd

Week 26 Day 1 (page 162)

1. point
2. joint
3. spoil
4. broil
5. hoist
6. topsoil
7. ploy
8. tinfoil
9. moist
10. cowboy

Week 26 Day 2 (page 163)

1. hoist
2. cowboy
3. topsoil
4. joint
5. spoil
6. point
7. moist
8. ploy
9. tinfoil
10. broil

Week 26 Day 3 (page 164)

Compound Words: tinfoil, cowboy, topsoil, voicemail, soybean
Not Compound Words: point, spoiled, ploys, moisten, broiling
ABC Order: broiling, cowboy, moisten, ploys, point, soybean, spoiled, tinfoil, topsoil, voicemail

Week 26 Day 4 (page 165)

Sentences should include bold words.

Week 26 Day 5 (page 166)

1. spoil
2. moist
3. tinfoil
4. hoist
5. cowboy
6. broil
7. topsoil
8. ploy
9. point
10. joint

Week 27 Day 1 (page 168)

1. soft
2. cost
3. lost
4. floss
5. frost
6. froth
7. cross
8. broth
9. cloth
10. gloss

Week 27 Day 2 (page 169)

1. cost
2. cloth
3. froth
4. cross
5. lost
6. soft
7. gloss
8. floss
9. broth
10. frost

Week 27 Day 3 (page 170)

1. crosses, crossing, crossed
   flosses, flossing, flossed
   glosses, glossing, glossed
2. frosted, frosting, frosty
3. softer, softest, softness
4. clothes, washcloth, dishcloth

Week 27 Day 4 (page 171)

Adjectives: bossy, frosty, pointy, oily, grouchy, cloudy

1. oily
2. grouchy
3. frosty
4. cloudy
5. bossy
6. pointy

Week 27 Day 5 (page 172)

1. soft
2. cost
3. lost
4. cross
5. frost
6. gloss
7. broth
8. cloth
9. froth
10. floss

Week 28 Day 1 (page 174)

1. sprawl
2. haul
3. fault
4. straw
5. scrawl
6. crawl
7. haunt
8. vault
9. flaunt
10. draw

Answer Key (cont.)

Week 28 Day 2 (page 175)

1.	flaunt	6.	scrawl
2.	haul	7.	haunt
3.	sprawl	8.	draw
4.	vault	9.	straw
5.	fault	10.	crawl

Week 28 Day 3 (page 176)

1. scrawls, scrawling, scrawled
   sprawls, sprawling, sprawled
2. haunts, haunting, haunted
   flaunts, flaunting, flaunted
3. drawing, drew, draws
4. hauling, hauls, hauled
5. crawler, crawling, crawled

Week 28 Day 4 (page 177)

Proper Nouns: Halloween, Boston, Austin, Paul, August
Common Nouns: autumn, father, frogs, lawn, straw
ABC Order: August, Austin, autumn, Boston, father, frogs, Halloween, lawn, Paul, straw

Week 28 Day 5 (page 178)

1.	crawl	6.	vault
2.	straw	7.	fault
3.	draw	8.	scrawl
4.	haul	9.	flaunt
5.	haunt	10.	sprawl

Week 29 Day 1 (page 180)

1.	scald	6.	swamp
2.	chalk	7.	want
3.	watch	8.	stalk
4.	wash	9.	bald
5.	also	10.	wand

Week 29 Day 2 (page 181)

1.	wash	6.	watch
2.	scald	7.	want
3.	also	8.	chalk
4.	swamp	9.	stalk
5.	bald	10.	wand

Week 29 Day 3 (page 182)

Compound Words: beanstalk, washcloth, chalkboard, stopwatch, crosswalk
Not Compound Words: flossing, wands, swampy, wanted, softness
ABC Order: beanstalk, chalkboard, crosswalk, flossing, softness, stopwatch, swampy, wands, wanted, washcloth

Week 29 Day 4 (page 183)

Sentences should include bold words.

Week 29 Day 5 (page 184)

1.	chalk	6.	bald
2.	wand	7.	swamp
3.	stalk	8.	want
4.	watch	9.	scald
5.	wash	10.	also

Week 30 Day 1 (page 186)

1.	skull	6.	should
2.	would	7.	bulb
3.	stood	8.	gulp
4.	crook	9.	sulk
5.	brook	10.	could

Week 30 Day 2 (page 187)

1.	sulk	6.	could
2.	gulp	7.	would
3.	crook	8.	skull
4.	should	9.	brook
5.	stood	10.	bulb

Week 30 Day 3 (page 188)

Present Tense Verbs: look, stand, cook, sulk, pull
Past Tense Verbs: took, gulped, pushed, shook, stood
ABC Order: cook, gulped, look, pull, pushed, shook, stand, stood, sulk, took

Week 30 Day 4 (page 189)

Sentences should include bold words.

Week 30 Day 5 (page 190)

1.	skull	6.	crook
2.	could	7.	bulb
3.	brook	8.	gulp
4.	should	9.	stood
5.	would	10.	sulk

Week 31 Day 1 (page 192)

1.	didn't	6.	doesn't
2.	can't	7.	they're
3.	wasn't	8.	I'll
4.	Who's	9.	it's
5.	we're	10.	You're

Week 31 Day 2 (page 193)

1.	can not, can't, n, o	6.	they are, they're, a
2.	did not, didn't, o	7.	was not, wasn't, o
3.	does not, doesn't, o	8.	we are, we're, a
4.	I will, I'll, w, i	9.	who is, who's, i
5.	it is, it's, i	10.	you are, you're, a

Week 31 Day 3 (page 194)

1.	your	5.	there
2.	you're	6.	they're
3.	it's	7.	who's
4.	its	8.	Whose

Week 31 Day 4 (page 195)

Sentences should include bold words.

Week 31 Day 5 (page 196)

Contractions with NOT: can't, wasn't, doesn't, didn't
Contractions with WILL: you'll, we'll, I'll
Contractions with ARE: they're, you're, we're
ABC Order: can't, didn't, doesn't, I'll, they're, wasn't, we'll, we're, you'll, you're

Week 32 Day 1 (page 198)

1.	carve	6.	scarf
2.	starve	7.	sharp
3.	shark	8.	smart
4.	spark	9.	march
5.	charm	10.	start

Week 32 Day 2 (page 199)

1.	smart	6.	start
2.	charm	7.	starve
3.	spark	8.	scarf
4.	carve	9.	march
5.	sharp	10.	shark

Answer Key (cont.)

Week 32 Day 3 (page 200)

1. starves, starving, starved
2. charms, charming, charmed
3. starts, starting, started
4. spark plug, sparked, sparkle
5. sharpness, sharpen, sharpest
6. marches, marched, marching

Week 32 Day 4 (page 201)

Adjectives: smart, sharp, large, hard, dark
Verbs: carve, starve, start, march, charm
ABC Order: carve, charm, dark, hard, large, march, sharp, smart, start, starve

Week 32 Day 5 (page 202)

1. carve
2. smart
3. starve
4. march
5. scarf
6. spark
7. sharp
8. charm
9. shark
10. start

Week 33 Day 1 (page 204)

1. store
2. sport
3. north
4. tour
5. four
6. pour
7. short
8. score
9. storm
10. porch

Week 33 Day 2 (page 205)

1. store
2. sports
3. tour
4. storm
5. short
6. north
7. porch
8. four
9. pour
10. score

Week 33 Day 3 (page 206)

Adjectives: stormy, sporty, thorny, bulky, mushy, pushy

1. thorny
2. stormy
3. pushy
4. sporty
5. mushy
6. bulky

Week 33 Day 4 (page 207)

Sentences should include bold words.

Week 33 Day 5 (page 208)

1. store
2. four
3. storm
4. porch
5. sport
6. north
7. score
8. pour
9. tour
10. short

Week 34 Day 1 (page 210)

1. shirt
2. chirp
3. squirt
4. thirst
5. third
6. stir
7. squirm
8. birth
9. twirl
10. first

Week 34 Day 2 (page 211)

1. twirl
2. squirm
3. stir
4. squirt
5. birth
6. first
7. shirt
8. chirp
9. third
10. thirst

Week 34 Day 3 (page 212)

1. twirls, twirling, twirled
2. squirts, squirting, squirted
3. squirms, squirming, squirmed
4. stirring, stirred, stirs
5. birthday, childbirth, births
6. thirsty, thirsts, thirsted

Week 34 Day 4 (page 213)

–ing: stirring, starring, scarring, slurring, spurring
–ed: stirred, starred, scarred, slurred, spurred

1. stirring
2. slurring
3. scarred
4. starred
5. spurring

Week 34 Day 5 (page 214)

1. first
2. birth
3. squirt
4. third
5. chirp
6. shirt
7. stir
8. thirst
9. twirl
10. squirm

Week 35 Day 1 (page 216)

1. perch
2. stern
3. blurb
4. clerk
5. blurt
6. church
7. slurp
8. burst
9. were
10. germs

Week 35 Day 2 (page 217)

1. burst
2. clerk
3. blurb
4. perch
5. stern
6. were
7. blurt
8. church
9. slurp
10. germs

Week 35 Day 3 (page 218)

Verbs: squirm, burst, slurp, chirp, blurt
Adverbs: sternly, firmly, softly, partly, hardly
ABC Order: blurt, burst, chirp, firmly, hardly, partly, slurp, softly, squirm, sternly

Week 35 Day 4 (page 219)

Nouns: teacher, player, reader, leader, farmer, builder

1. farmer
2. teacher
3. builder
4. reader
5. player
6. leader

Week 35 Day 5 (page 220)

1. church
2. burst
3. perch
4. germs
5. slurp
6. clerk
7. were
8. blurb
9. stern
10. blurt

Week 36 Day 1 (page 222)

1. twenty
2. happy
3. jelly
4. pretty
5. penny
6. puppy
7. funny
8. silly
9. candy
10. ugly

Answer Key (cont.)

Week 36 Day 2 (page 223)

1. funny
2. pretty
3. candy
4. happy
5. silly
6. ugly
7. penny
8. jelly
9. twenty
10. puppy

Week 36 Day 3 (page 224)

Plural Nouns: puppies, pennies, candies, bunnies, jellies
More: uglier, prettier, funnier, sillier, sloppier
Most: ugliest, prettiest, funniest, silliest, sloppiest

Week 36 Day 4 (page 225)

Sentences should include bold words.

Week 36 Day 5 (page 226)

1. happy
2. puppy
3. twenty
4. candy
5. penny
6. funny
7. jelly
8. pretty
9. ugly
10. silly

Unit Assessments

At the end of each unit, use the corresponding quiz to determine what students have learned. Ask students to spell the two words. Then, have students write the sentence. Say the words and sentence slowly, repeating as often as needed. The bolded words were studied in the unit.

Unit	Phonetic Pattern	Words	Sentence
1	short *a* words	bask, mast	You can **ask** for a pink **cast**.
2	more short *a* words	ramp, sand	Can you give me a **hand** with the **plant**?
3	short *i* words	sift, silk	Did you put **milk** on the **list**?
4	short *e* words	bent, kept	Beth **felt** sick, so she **left** and **went** to bed.
5	short *o* and short *u* words	pump, rust	What **does** the **pond** look like at **dusk**?
6	–*ck* ending	cluck, stock	He had a **black speck** on his pants.
7	silent letters	limb, wren	Can you show me how to **knit** a neck **wrap**?
8	long *a* and long *i* ending in silent *e*	blame, slime	You will need a **knife** and **plate**.
9	long *o* and long *u* ending in silent *e*	clone, flume	Why is a **plume** of **smoke** coming out of the **stove**?
10	*r* blends	grand, trust	Dad lets Greg **drive** his **truck**.
11	consonant digraphs	crunch, trash	Did you have **fresh shrimp** for **lunch**?
12	soft *c* and soft *g* words	page, truce	A **slice** of ham does not cost ten **cents**.
13	–*ng* and –*nk* endings	drank, stung	**Thank** you for **bringing** me a hot **drink**.
14	long *a* vowel team *ay*	bray, sway	We can **stay** and **play** with some **clay**.
15	long *a* vowel team *ai*	drain, snail	I helped Mom **paint** the **chair** on our deck.
16	long *e* vowel team *ea*	cheat, streak	You can **clean** your feet in the **stream**.
7	long *e* vowel team *ee*	breed, greet	I love to **sleep** on my **green sheets**.
	long *i* patterns *igh, ild, ind*	kind, blight	We helped the **child find** his seat on the **flight**.
	long *o* vowel team *oa*	cloak, gloat	The swim **coach** told us to **float** in the pool.

Unit Assessments (cont.)

Unit	Phonetic Pattern	Words	Sentence
20	long *o* vowel team *ow*	crow, rainbow	Do you **know** how to **throw** a ball of **snow**?
21	long *o* patterns *old*, *olt*, *ost*	bold, host	**Hold** the sheet with **both** hands when you **fold** it.
22	long *u* pattern *oo*	proof, stool	She **scooped** the **smooth** ice cream with a **spoon**.
23	long *u* patterns *eu*, *ew*, and *ui*	brew, shrew	Is it **true** that you **threw** away some of the **fruit**?
24	*ou* diphthong	mound, pouch	We **crouched** near the **ground** to see the **sprouting** plants.
25	*ow* diphthong	frown, howl	The **clown** handed out **flowers** to a **crowd** of kids.
26	*oi/oy* diphthongs	coin, join	If you **broil** the meat too long it won't be **moist**.
27	/ô/ pattern with *o*	loft, sloth	How much does it **cost** for three **soft cloths**?
28	/ô/ pattern with *au* and *aw*	daunt, shawl	I saw a gray cat **crawl** into the **straw**.
29	/ô/ pattern with *wa* and *al*	swan, wasp	Kim **also wants** to walk to the **swamp** with us.
30	schwa sounds	pulp, shook	Jack **stood** in line with me, but Jim **would** not.
31	contractions	she's, we'll	I **didn't** say **you're** mean.
32	*r*-controlled vowels with *ar*	chart, snarl	**Sharks** could **starve** without **sharp** teeth.
33	*r*-controlled vowels with *our*, *or*, and *ore*	snore, torch	We sat on the **porch** and watched the **storm**.
34	*r*-controlled vowels with *ir*	birch, skirt	She **squirted** blue paint on my **shirt first**!
35	*r*-controlled vowels with *er* and *ur*	churn, herself	The **clerk** was very **stern** when we **burst** into the store.
36	–*y* endings	bunny, handy	**Silly puppies** make me **happy**.

Spelling Categories

Spelling Category	Spelling Pattern	Unit
Short Vowels	short *a* words	1
	more short *a* words	2
	short *i* words	3
	short *e* words	4
	short *o* and short *u* words	5
Consonant Digraphs and Blends	–*ck* ending	6
	r blends	10
	consonant digraphs	11
	–*ng* and –*nk* endings	13
Silent, Soft, and Missing Letters	silent letters	7
	long *a* and long *i* ending in silent *e*	8
	long *o* and long *u* ending in silent *e*	9
	soft *c* and soft *g* words	12
	contractions	31
Long Vowels	long *a* vowel team *ay*	14
	long *a* vowel team *ai*	15
	long *e* vowel team *ea*	16
	long *e* vowel team *ee*	17
	long *i* patterns *igh, ild, ind*	18
	long *o* vowel team *oa*	19
	long *o* vowel team *ow*	20
	long *o* patterns *old, olt, ost*	21
	long *u* pattern *oo*	22
	long *u* patterns *eu, ew,* and *ui*	23
Ambiguous Vowels	*ou* diphthong	24
	ow diphthong	25
	oi/oy diphthongs	26
	/ô/ pattern with *o*	27
	/ô/ pattern with *au* and *aw*	28
	/ô/ pattern with *wa* and *al*	29
	schwa sounds	30
r-Controlled Vowels	*r*-controlled vowels with *ar*	32
	r-controlled vowels with *our, or,* and *ore*	33
	r-controlled vowels with *ir*	34
	r-controlled vowels with *er* and *ur*	35
Final Syllables	–*y* endings	36

Digital Resources

Accessing the Digital Resources

The digital resources can be downloaded by following these steps:

1. Go to **www.tcmpub.com/digital**

2. Sign in or create an account.

3. Click **Redeem Content** and enter the ISBN number, located on page 2 and the back cover, into the appropriate field on the website.

4. Respond to the prompts using the book to view your account and available digital content.

5. Choose the digital resources you would like to download. You can download all the files at once, or you can download a specific group of files.

ISBN:
9781425833107

Please note: Some files provided for download have large file sizes. Download times for these larger files will vary based on your download speed.

 ## Contents of the Digital Resources

Teaching Resources Folder

- Additional Spelling Activities (page 7)

- Additional Word Lists (below, on, and above grade level)

- Unit Overview Pages

Assessments Folder

- Analysis Charts separated by spelling category

- Unit Assessments (pages 237–238)

- Assessment Reproducible